WIRED THAT WAY

THE COMPREHENSIVE PERSONALITY PLAN

BASED ON THE TEACHINGS OF

MARITA LITTAUER & FLORENCE LITTAUER

Revell

a division of Baker Publishing Group
Grand Rapids, Michigan

© 2006 by Marita Littauer

Published by Revell
a division of Baker Publishing Group
PO Box 6287, Grand Rapids, MI 49516-6287
www.revellbooks.com

Revell edition published 2014
ISBN 978-0-8007-2538-9

Previously published by Regal Books

Printed in the United States of America

Library of Congress Control Number: 2014955801

Unless otherwise indicated, Scripture quotations are from the Holy Bible, New International Version®. NIV®. Copyright © 1973, 1978, 1984 by Biblica, Inc.™ Used by permission of Zondervan. All rights reserved worldwide. www.zondervan.com

Scripture quotations labeled KJV are from the King James Version of the Bible.

Scripture quotations labeled NASB are from the New American Standard Bible®, copyright © 1960, 1962, 1963, 1968, 1971, 1972, 1973, 1975, 1977, 1995 by The Lockman Foundation. Used by permission.

Writing contributed by Tamie Vervoorn

CONTENTS

CHAPTER 1

FOUNDATION AND BACKGROUND

Can you think of people in your life whom you'd like to change? People who are too demanding, too talkative, too introspective or who just don't have it together? Do you ever just want to walk away from a relationship because communication seems impossible, and it seems like the other person will never change?

But are they really the ones who need to change? As Marita Littauer suggests in *Wired That Way*, "Once we give up trying to change the people in our life—and accept that they are just wired that way—we can begin to understand others and improve our relationships with them. Likewise, when we are able to grasp the way we are wired, we can use that knowledge to grow beyond our natural tendencies and become better and more balanced individuals" (page 12).

We all wrestle with things that we want to change about ourselves, but often we feel frustrated because we don't know where to begin. Understanding the way people are wired is essential for living in our strengths, growing through our weaknesses, and building better relationships. Such knowledge affords us greater possibilities for being "at peace with everyone" (Romans 12:18) as well as for being at peace with ourselves.

- Let's begin by taking a look at ourselves. Describe a situation in which you tried to change someone with whom you worked, lived or had a close relationship. Maybe that person had a personality quirk that annoyed you, or perhaps you subtly—for whatever reason—tried to make him or her more like yourself. What was the outcome of your attempts?

- In your life today, who do you have a hard time relating to or communicating with? What about that person would you like to change?

- What does Matthew 7:3 say about judging the apparent flaws of others?

- Look closely at the areas of weakness in your own life. Do you have behavior patterns or character traits that seem to sabotage your relationships?

Discovering Your Personality Type

Sometimes these flaws and weaknesses have less to do with sin or irresponsibility in our lives than with our actual Personality. "We all come with our own Personality, determined before birth within our individual genetic makeup," Marita writes. "They are inborn Personality traits—the way we are wired" (pages 12-13). And each of our Personality types is prone to various strengths and weaknesses. (Note: If you haven't yet picked up a copy of the *Wired That Way Personality Profile* and discovered your own unique Personality type, now would be a great time to do this.)

- Look up Psalm 139. What does it say about the way God "wired" you?

Isn't it comforting to know that God didn't make us clones of one another? Although we do possess general similarities in our Personalities, He fashioned each one of us uniquely so that we might glorify Him and complement one another! In this study guide, we will take a deeper look at each of our Personalities in order to determine how we can develop healthier relationships with others. It is our hope that this guide will give you the tools you need to improve your relationships with others and solve any relational problems you may be experiencing with others.

- Write out Philippians 2:4. What does this verse communicate about healthy relationships?

- What key relationship(s) with others in your life could benefit from a better understanding of the way you (and they!) are wired?

- Write out Romans 1:8, and then write down what you think this verse says about how God sees those of us who are in Christ (even with all of our quirks and shortcomings).

This, of course, is not an excuse for sin, but a reminder of God's grace. He sees us as He sees Christ. Therefore, we do not need to feel condemned for the parts of our Personality that need work. God is in the business of refining (or sanctifying) us to make us more like Him. Only through communion with Him and His Word can we mature. Only in Him will we see the true redemption of our Personalities.

- Celebrate Jesus' sanctifying work in you by writing out the following verses:

John 17:17-19

1 Thessalonians 5:23

Our environment, of course, also shapes our Personalities, but as Marita says in *Wired That Way,* "the basics are predetermined" (page 12). This ought to be a refreshing thought to those who may have struggled all their lives to be neat and tidy, but whose Personality actually predisposes them toward being a bit cluttered and scattered—or who have felt inadequate for not being dynamic conversationalists or powerful leaders, not knowing that their prepackaged Personality determines much of who they are and how they behave.

Marita says the following about how organization does not come easy for her: "As a Popular Sanguine, I am not really very organized, but as a business owner and a professional speaker, I have had to learn to get organized. So, yes, I am organized, but it is something I struggle with every day of my life."

Who Are You, Anyway?

When we understand our God-given personality types, we can better determine the changes we need to make to become the people that we want to be without beating ourselves up over who we're not.

- After reading the descriptions of each Personality given in chapter 1, which one did you most identify with?

- Did you have any "a-ha" moments when you read these descriptions, recognizing the people you live and work with? Using the space below, see if you can identify the Personality type of several of your close friends. (It might also be fun for you to have them take the Personality Profile with you as well!)

- If you have taken the Personality Profile, what did it reveal to you about your dominant Personality type? Are you more of a Popular Sanguine, a Powerful Choleric, a Perfect Melancholy or a Peaceful Phlegmatic?

Popular Sanguine

Keeping in mind the description of the Popular Sanguine as given in *Wired That Way*, let's review some of the key traits that might show up in someone with a dominant Popular Sanguine personality.

- What are the key strengths and weaknesses of the Popular Sanguine?

- What kind of people does the Popular Sanguine like to be around? Who don't they like (or feel liked by)?

- What kind of leadership might you expect from a Popular Sanguine?

- What might be an instant indicator that you've just met a Popular Sanguine?

Powerful Choleric

Let's review the dominant traits of the Powerful Choleric Personality type.

- What is a primary desire of the Powerful Choleric?

- What, generally, are the Powerful Choleric's emotional needs? How might you adjust your approach (knowing what you now know) to meet the needs of a significant Powerful Choleric in your life?

- What is the Powerful Choleric's typical reaction to stress?

- How might you immediately recognize a Powerful Choleric?

Perfect Melancholy

Let's review the unique traits of the Perfect Melancholy personality type.

- What might the Perfect Melancholy's motto be?

- What tends to make Perfect Melancholies depressed, and what are they generally afraid of?

- How would a Perfect Melancholy be valuable in a work situation?

- How could the Perfect Melancholy's strengths be beneficial in your own life?

- How could you easily recognize a Perfect Melancholy?

Peaceful Phlegmatic

In *Wired That Way*, Marita tells us that the Peaceful Phlegmatic might be the hardest Personality to recognize. Let's review some of the key traits of the Peaceful Phlegmatic.

- What kind of person is the Peaceful Phlegmatic? Why are Peaceful Phlegmatics not as easy to identify as the other Personalities?

- What are the Peaceful Phlegmatic's key strengths? Now think of a possible Peaceful Phlegmatic person in your own life. Why do you enjoy being around that person?

- What Personality do Peaceful Phlegmatics tend to marry, and why?

- How can a person's posture indicate that he or she might be a Peaceful Phlegmatic?

Relating It to Relationships

As you think about your unique Personality traits—and those of your coworkers, family members and friends—you can start to apply this new knowledge to key areas in your life. The Personalities can provide you with a fantastic tool for interacting with people and can even solve relationship problems that naturally crop up when Personality types clash.

- Do you see how relationships in each of these key areas have been affected by the Personalities of those with whom you interact every day?

- With these Personality differences in mind, how can you change your approach toward a coworker, boss, family member or friend?

In the sidebar on page 23 of *Wired That Way*, Kathryn Robbins makes a noteworthy point: "What you want to become is a well-balanced individual who is living in his or her strengths, not wallowing in weaknesses."

- Think about your dominant Personality. What is a strength that you have been operating in and that you are grateful to possess? Also think about and write down one area in which you would like to make improvements.

- Read Ephesians 4:2-3,15-16. What do these verses say about how we ought to approach one another?

- Applying these Scriptures and what you have read in *Wired That Way* to your relationships, list a few ways in which you might encourage your Popular Sanguine family, friends and/or coworkers:

- How would you go about encouraging the Powerful Cholerics in your life?

- How would you go about encouraging the Perfect Melancholies in your life?

- How would you go about encouraging the Peaceful Phlegmatics in your life?

- Which Personality type do you feel you clash with most and why?

• What could you do to be at peace with people who have that type of Personality?

What Does the Word Say?

Within the Bible's pages, you can learn a lot about relationships and how to relate to others. In fact, the sharpest wisdom for all of human interaction can be found in the Word of God. Take some time to pick up your Bible and study the following verses. As you read and write down the verses listed below, reflect on how each verse teaches you how to deal with Personalities that are different from your own. After reading each verse, write down your thoughts about it.

Matthew 5:9

Matthew 22:39

Mark 9:50

John 13:34

Romans 12:10

Putting It into Practice

Before moving on, stop and ask God to help you have a better understanding of people who have Personalities different from your own. Ask Him to help you be more loving, more compassionate, more confident and more at ease (or whatever your particular need is) with people whom you find difficult. Ask Him to help you thrive in your strengths and transform your weaknesses. Commit these concerns to Him now, at the beginning of this workbook, and He will give you the grace to change!

VISIBLE CLUES

In chapter 2 of *Wired That Way*, Marita illuminates a simple fact that has been confirmed by researchers: "People will be more likely to respond favorably to you if they like you" (page 26). As Christians, while we don't want to become people-pleasers—and the goal isn't necessarily to be liked by everyone (although that would be nice)—we do want to have a positive influence in people's lives. From that place, we are able to speak the truth to people; specifically the truth about Jesus Christ.

The apostle Paul wrote, "I have become all things to all men so that by all possible means I might save some" (1 Corinthians 9:22). It would be a pretty good guess to assume that Paul wasn't out to win a popularity contest, but he seemed to be very intentional about identifying with those to whom he ministered. In a similar way, we also can discover the needs and Personalities of others so that we can be better equipped to relate to them.

Is there someone in your life—whether an acquaintance, a close friend or a family member—with whom you'd like to share Jesus? Would understanding his or her Personality help you to do that more effectively? Can you identify his or her primary Personality? Secondary Personality?

We will have a far more significant place of influence in people's lives when we learn to communicate with them according to their Personality's needs. They will be more likely to be drawn to us. As John Maxwell states in his book *Twenty-five Ways to Win with People*, "Those who add to us, draw us to them. Those who subtract, cause us to withdraw."[1]

Changing Your Approach

In her story about Joanne, the receptionist at her new dentist's office, Marita notes that she took the time to identify Joanne's Personality and chat with her, during which time they connected. To truly connect with someone, we have to *take the time*. It is possible to identify a person's Personality after only a brief encounter and to respond to him or her accordingly. However, to truly understand and connect with someone, we must take the time to talk to and find out more about him or her.

Employees and employers, husbands and wives, parents and children so often butt heads because they are trying to change one another. "Wouldn't it be great if everyone with whom you interacted actually liked you?" Marita states. "While you can't change those other people, you can figure out their Personality and then change the way you approach them based on that information" (page 28).

- Think of someone you have wanted to change. What are some visible clues as to what his or her Personality type is? How does he or she dress? What distinct mannerisms do you notice? What is his or her preference in regard to personal space?

- In what significant ways do you think he or she differs from you? Being honest here, can you identify the specific thing(s) that you have wanted to change about that person?

Philippians 2:4 tells us to look out for the interests of others and not merely our own. Is there an emotional need that you can meet for that person in order to help him or her respond more favorably to you? If we can learn to notice the Personalities swirling all around us, we can actually improve our relationships, one person at a time.

Picking Out Personalities at a Glance

Popular Sanguine

"One of the greatest fears of the Popular Sanguine is that they might blend in—that they might not be noticed" (page 30 in *Wired That Way*). We can see from what Marita writes that expressing personal style and individuality is very important for Popular Sanguines.

• What light does this shed on your observations of your Popular Sanguine friends (or on yourself)?

• Two key words that Marita gives us for identifying a Popular Sanguine in a crowd are "loud" and "open." If you are a Popular Sanguine, have you ever felt bad for having these traits? Have you ever felt that others have shunned you because of them?

• If you're not a Popular Sanguine, have you ever been the one to shush or reprimand a Popular Sanguine?

As we come to better understand the Popular Sanguine Personality, we can accept that we don't need to feel bad about or be mad at them because they have these *loud* and *open* characteristics. After all, as Marita says, "We Popular Sanguines save the customer service representatives from boredom"—and probably save a lot of customer relations that would be lost if the person were dealing with another Personality!

• Do you know anyone who is a "No Test Needed" Popular Sanguine?

Because of their open nature, Popular Sanguines sometimes say *too* much. With maturity and practice, however, the Popular Sanguine can overcome this weakness and keep from embarrassing themselves and offending others.

• What do the Proverbs say about guarding our speech? Look up the following verses and write down a quick summary of the main points.

Proverbs 10:32

Proverbs 11:13

Proverbs 16:28

• If you're a Popular Sanguine, or if you're close with someone who reveals TMI (*too much information*) about his or her own life or the lives of others, what can you do to encourage more discreet behavior?

Popular Sanguines have open, affectionate body language, and other Personalities can learn to appreciate this quality (and even begin to express affection more effectively themselves) by taking cues from their Popular Sanguine friends, family members and colleagues. Of course, Popular Sanguines need to learn when open affection is appropriate and when it might be overwhelming to other different Personality types.

Perfect Melancholy
Standing at the opposite end of the spectrum from Popular Sanguines are Perfect Melancholies. Perfect Melancholies typically have a quiet voice, closed body language, greater respect for those around them, a need for personal space, and a much more organized personal environment. Already, we can see how there could be misunderstandings between Popular Sanguines and Perfect Melancholies. In seeking to understand these basic differences, however, we can apply what we know to our relationships and work to improve them.

• Read 1 Corinthians 13:1-7. It appears that all the Personalities are represented in verses 1-3—those who speak eloquently, those who are very knowledgeable, those who are bold, and those who will sacrifice themselves for someone else. What does verse 4 say love *is*, and what does verse 5 say it *is not*?

• What does verse 7 say love always *does*?

• How might having an understanding of the Personalities help you to have more patience and kindness toward people with Personalities that are the opposite of yours? How might it keep you from being easily angered with them?

• The Perfect Melancholy tends to have a closed mouth and a closed life. Why might these characteristics tend to isolate Perfect Melancholies from others? How might Perfect Melancholies allow others "in" to their lives more and become more open and caring?

In Marita's story about her Perfect Melancholy friend with the green suit, she illustrates how, in regard to personal style, the Perfect Melancholy enjoys lasting value and quality, while the Popular Sanguine likes variety and change and an eccentric flare. She concludes by saying, "Neither view is right nor wrong—they are just different" (page 34).

• Read Romans 14:1-19. What does Paul have to say about the "negotiables" in life?

- How are we to treat the different views and tastes of others?

- Perfect Melancholies need peace and quiet. In *Wired That Way,* Marita shares how her husband, a Perfect Melancholy, enjoys it when she "plays the silence." If you have a Perfect Melancholy spouse, child, roommate or colleague, list specific examples of how/when you can do this. What can you do to show respect for the Perfect Melancholy's need for personal space?

- If you are a Perfect Melancholy, when would be an appropriate time to raise your voice a little and throw off the constraints of quietness? (See Psalms 9:11; 18:6; 20:5; 26:7; 27:6.)

- If you're not a Perfect Melancholy, have you ever been offended or hurt by a Perfect Melancholy's lack of words or lack of physical affection toward you? If so, using what you now know about his or her Personality, can you reinterpret the situation(s) to positively reflect Personality differences? Write about it briefly in the space provided.

Powerful Choleric

Powerful Cholerics are focused and intense, do everything with a purpose, and tend to have a shorter fuse than everyone else. According to Marita, "If the Powerful Cholerics in your life are a positive influence in your life, they will bring a sense of energy and excitement with them. If they are a negative influence in your life, they will bring a sense of energy with them, but not the good kind—it will bring stress and tension. Regardless of the effects Powerful Cholerics have on you personally, they will never leave any doubt that they are currently occupying the same room as you are" (page 39 in *Wired That Way*).

- Considering what Marita writes abut the physical expressions of the Powerful Choleric, cite a few specific circumstances in which a Powerful Choleric might need to curb these actions when dealing with more sensitive individuals.

- Write out the following verses with a brief comment as to what a Powerful Choleric can learn from each of them.

Proverbs 11:17

Proverbs 15:1

Hosea 11:4

Matthew 11:29

Galatians 5:22-23

- If you're not a Powerful Choleric, you can probably remember a time when someone of this Personality type made you feel hurt, rejected or threatened. Reviewing those circumstances—and that person— through different lenses (namely, an understanding of the way the Powerful Choleric is wired), how might your perception of that person's behavior be different now?

Are you a Powerful Choleric? If so, don't feel condemned for your strong personality. After all, God wired you that way! But consider Ephesians 4:2: "Be completely humble and gentle; be patient, bearing with one another in love." Toward whom do you need to exercise more gentleness and humility?

Peaceful Phlegmatic

Because Peaceful Phlegmatics have the least obvious Personality traits, they are often the most difficult of the Personalites to identify. Marita calls them the "chameleon" of the Personalities: "Because their traits are not as extreme, it is easier for the Peaceful Phlegmatic to be flexible to whatever the task at hand demands. Yet this in itself is a clue that you're dealing with this Personality type" (page 42).

People who are Peaceful Phlegmatics are naturally flexible and tend to go with the flow. Like the apostle Paul, they "become all things to all men" (1 Corinthians 9:22). Of course, this doesn't mean that they should allow themselves to lose their sense of self or who God created them to be. Marita shares the story of one friend, the vice president of operations for a nationwide ministry, who wore herself out doing that: "All day long, she had to pull from the depths of her resources to be someone whom she was not" (page 42).

- In what areas might the Peaceful Phlegmatic try to be and do what everyone else needs? In what way might the Peaceful Phlegmatic try to fill a role that's better suited to another Personality?

- How can the other Personalities watch out for the Peaceful Phlegmatics in their lives to see that they don't get walked on, left out or forgotten? How can others show Peaceful Phlegmatics how grateful they are for the sense of balance and peace that they bring to everyone around them?

- Marita says that the Peaceful Phlegmatic's unwritten rule is, "Why stand when you can sit; why sit when you can lie down" (page 44). *Rest* is a biblical principle, but the Peaceful Phlegmatic might need to guard against *laziness*. List the advice, admonitions and warnings given in each of the following Scripture verses:

Proverbs 10:4

Proverbs 13:4

Proverbs 21:5

Colossians 3:23

2 Thessalonians 3:8-10

- List a few creative ways that other Personalities can encourage Peaceful Phlegmatics to be productive without offending their peacemaking nature or strong iron-will.

Blind Date

Psalm 139:13-14 states, "You created my inmost being; you knit me together in my mother's womb. I praise you because I am fearfully and wonderfully made; your works are wonderful, I know that full well." God wired each one of us before we were even born. For that, we can be grateful—and we can even have a sense of peace, value and identity. Isn't it wonderful to know that the God of the universe created you just the way He wanted you and that He has every intention of using you and your unique Personality to do great things?

- Read Marita's "blind date" example at the end of chapter 2 and then describe yourself in three short sentences, as if to someone you have just met.

    1.

    2.

    3.

- Ask a close friend or family member to describe you in the same way. In the space provided, write down what your friend or relative says about you.

- Are there any discrepancies? Are you the Personality that you originally thought you were?

Putting It into Practice

Let's finish by praying this simple prayer:

Dear Father, thank You that You have made me unique and that You were intimately involved in creating me. Thank You that I am "fearfully and wonderfully made." Thank You that You created me to fulfill a special role on this earth—and that my God-given Personality plays a big part in that.

Help me to learn from You and from others how to be mature and balanced. Help me to learn how to really love others as I love myself. I want to see people through Your eyes, as the unique individuals You've created them to be. Please help me, Holy Spirit, to act on what I've learned. I commit to looking out for the needs of those around me and to being selfless—like You were, Jesus—that I might bless them and show Your love to them.

In Jesus' name, Amen.

Note

1. John Maxwell, *Twenty-five Ways to Win with People* (Nashville, TN: Nelson Business, 2005), n.p.

CHAPTER 3

STRENGTHS AND WEAKNESSES

Now that you have identified your Personality, it's time to discover your strengths and learn how to maximize them. In this chapter you'll also take a moment to honestly evaluate your weaknesses and learn how to diminish them.

Be True to Yourself

Understanding the Personalities is all about relationships. Understanding ourselves is good; finding healing and confidence through that understanding is even better; but what's best about all of this is what it brings to our *relationships*. No relationship can be true and whole while facades are still up.

As Marita states in *Wired That Way*, we want to refine our Personalities, not reject them. She gives examples of two people (the salesman she dated and Debi) who, for different reasons, did such extreme makeovers of their original Personalities that it was hard to tell who they really were!

- Have you ever met someone like the salesman Marita dated—someone who seemed too perfect and not authentic? How did you feel about that person?

• Read Debi's story on page 51 of *Wired That Way*. Have you ever tried to conform to meet the expectations of people and society? Perhaps you're recognizing and coming out of that phase right now! Why is living like that so painful and destructive? What are the dangers of trying to be someone you're not?

"Trying to be someone you are not is emotionally expensive," Marita says. "[It] is exhausting, and the damage often comes in the form of stress-related illnesses" (pages 50-51). Most people have a faulty perception of what the perfect man or woman, husband or wife, student or professional should be. When we place expectations on ourselves and others to become what we think is "perfect," usually we do more harm than good. We end up feeling worse about ourselves, alienating other people, and making ourselves less able to relate to others—less *real*.

• What does Romans 12:2 say about conforming to the world's expectations? If this is true, how are we to be transformed?

We need to be transformed by the renewing of our minds! We need to think rightly, to think *biblically* about ourselves, and about others. *Then* we can know—and rightly do—the will of God. That's what this study is about, learning to correct our thinking and be transformed into who God always meant for us to be. And He promises that if we seek Him, we can be assured that He will transform us. We don't have to strive to be someone we're not!

• Write out the following Scriptures in the spaces provided.

2 Corinthians 4:16

Colossians 3:10

• What do these verses communicate about this transforming work that God is doing in us?

Personality Strengths and Weaknesses

Let's follow Marita's advice as we dive into this next section: "As you review the following sections, think about not only which of these specific traits fit you but also the people with whom you interact on a daily basis. How can you use this knowledge to grow? How can you use it to adjust your expectations of others?" (page 52).

Popular Sanguine
Marita sometimes tells the following story about her naturally inquisitive nature:

> One day I was speaking at a church in Paducah, Kentucky. They had assigned to me a "shepherd," a person who takes care of the speaker and makes sure I get to where I belong at the appointed time. My shepherd was a Popular Sanguine, too. When break time came, she was nowhere to be found. Coffee stations were set up throughout the meeting area, but I prefer tea. I carry my own tea bags, so I went off in search of some hot water. I was directed to go down a hall and to make a left through the double doors and into the kitchen. "There someone can help you," I was told.
>
> I got to the kitchen, but no one was there. I looked around and saw a microwave oven near a sink. Next to the microwave were stacks of Styrofoam cups. I now had everything I needed to make tea. I put the water in the cup, put the cup in the microwave, and set the timer for two minutes. As I stood waiting for the water to boil, I noticed that just above the microwave, a cupboard door was open about three-quarters of an inch. Inside I could see packages of individually wrapped Saltine crackers. Without thinking about it, I reached up, opened the cupboard, and took a look. That was when one of the church staff walked in and caught me, the speaker, snooping through the church's provisions. "May I help you find something?" the person asked, to which I could only reply, "No, I was just looking" as I sheepishly closed the door.

Do you have a story about a Popular Sanguine whose "curious, inquisitive nature" got him or her (or *you*!) into trouble or an embarrassing situation? One of the Popular Sanguine's strengths is to turn work into play.

This can be a great asset! As Proverbs 15:15 says, "The cheerful heart has a continual feast." Popular Sanguines can make their coworkers the guests of honor at the party—*every day*!

- If you're a Popular Sanguine, how can you use this strength, in a practical way, to "infect" or motivate others with your joy and enthusiasm?

- Write out Matthew 18:3 and Galatians 5:22. What do they have to say about having a fun, joyful spirit?

Another strength that Popular Sanguines have to offer is their ability to make friends easily. And who doesn't need a friend? If you're feeling lonely, look for a Popular Sanguine to cheer you up. Ask him or her to tell you about himself or herself, and you'll be sure to make a "new best friend"!

- Think of someone whom you encounter in your weekly routine (at work, on campus, at the gym) who seems to be in need of a friend. Find a way to reach out to that person and flex some of your Popular Sanguine muscle. (Powerful Cholerics, Perfect Melancholies and Peaceful Phlegmatics: This one is for you, too!) Write down that person's name or description:

While Popular Sanguines have many wonderful strengths, their weaknesses often include being egotistical, talking too much, wasting time at work, and being fickle and forgetful.

- Can you think of a time when you felt self-sufficient and either refused help or never asked for any help, only to find yourself later in a bind? What happened and how was it a humbling situation?

- How does 2 Samuel 22:28 warn against thinking too highly of yourself?

- How does Proverbs 11:2 warn of this same thing?

- What does Proverbs 14:23 say about too much talk at work?

- If you're a Popular Sanguine, are there people whom you have treated poorly because they have been "out of sight, out of mind"? How might these friends and family members feel about your lack of contact? What can you do to show them you still care?

While making a "new best friend" every day might be great for you, remember these words of wisdom: "A man of many companions may come to ruin, but there is a friend who sticks closer than a brother" (Proverbs 18:24).

Powerful Choleric
Powerful Cholerics exude confidence and drive. They are goal-oriented and eager to get the job done.

- How were Jesus' Powerful Choleric qualities displayed throughout the book of Luke (see 9:51; 13:31-33), as He resolutely made His way to Jerusalem? What about what we read about Jesus in Matthew 16:21-23?

Despite her knowledge of the Personalities, Kathleen was still surprised with this encounter:

> After presenting workshops on the Personalities at my office, I occasionally find myself in the middle of conflicts as my coworkers try to understand the other person's point of view.
>
> On one occasion, my coworker Cheryl asked if I would go with her to talk with one of our colleagues, Roger, because he had said some hurtful things to her and she wanted to resolve the situation. Being a close friend of his, I called Roger to set up a meeting time. He was a strong Powerful Choleric, while Cheryl was Powerful Choleric/Popular Sanguine.
>
> The three of us met together. Cheryl told her side of the story to Roger and then stated how she had interpreted his comments. I quickly said, "I am sure that if Roger knew that he hurt your feelings, he would be the first to apologize." I gave him a look that said, "Please realize that you said the wrong thing to Cheryl."
>
> Roger said, "Yes, Cheryl, I apologize if you misunderstood what I meant to say." And then he excused himself from the interchange.

Sometimes, that is about as much of an apology as you can expect to get from a Powerful Choleric!

• Whether you are a Powerful Choleric or not, what can you learn from Jesus' determination and commitment to His goal?

• Given what you have learned thus far about the Personalities, what is one goal you will strive to reach this week with regard to improving your relationships? (It can be a goal that involves one person in particular or a goal that concerns people in general.)

The Powerful Choleric excels in emergencies and is an exceptional leader and organizer. As Marita notes, "Inside every Powerful Choleric is a hero just waiting for a chance to show what he or she is made of. In an emergency, the Powerful Choleric's quick thinking, fast action, sheer guts and fortitude often save the day." Do you know anyone like that?

- What would make a Powerful Choleric who is living in his or her strengths a great boss, coach or group leader?

- What can be the downside for the Powerful Choleric, given his or her ability to be so strong and self-sufficient?

Another aspect of Powerful Cholerics' Personality that doesn't win them friends is their tendency to be unsympathetic. Powerful Cholerics often have a difficult time expressing empathy.

- Again, Ephesians 4:2 speaks to this negative characteristic. How does it say we are to bear with others?

- Look up the Scripture passages below that address this issue. Meditate on these passages and then write down how you can begin to live out your call to be loving and compassionate.

Psalm 86:15

Hosea 6:6

Zechariah 7:9

- In the book of Job, how did Job's friends prove unsympathetic in his time of need?

If you are a Powerful Choleric and struggle with being unsympathetic toward those you work with or live with, you might need to repent and ask for forgiveness from those individuals. If this is the case, think of it as an achievement—a chance to conquer another weakness that you wrestle with: the unwillingness to apologize!

Perfect Melancholy

The Perfect Melancholy is perhaps the Personality that best exemplifies Romans 12:15: "Rejoice with those who rejoice; mourn with those who mourn." Perfect Melancholies are sensitive and highly sympathetic toward others. Because they don't make a new friend every day, they can be, as Proverbs 18:24 says, that friend who "sticks closer than a brother." Perfect Melancholies are also deeply passionate, creative, and tend to be well-organized and detail-oriented.

- How does this natural sense of order in the Perfect Melancholy reflect God's character (see 1 Corinthians 14:33)?

Because Perfect Melancholies are sensitive and have a deep concern for others, they need to be careful to guard their hearts (see Proverbs 4:23) so as not to become overburdened by other people's emotions and trials. Yes, in Galatians 6:2 the apostle Paul says to "carry each other's burdens," but he goes on to say that we're all responsible for our own loads (see v. 5). So, while Perfect Melancholies might do a great job of bearing others' burdens, other Personalities need to be sure that they don't push the weight of their woes onto the hearts of their listening friends.

Perhaps it is this tendency to take on more emotional weight than they should that leads Perfect Melancholies to feel more depressed and moody than others—a weakness that often pushes people away. If you are a Perfect Melancholy and find this to be true in your life, realize that other people are affected by your emotions, too! Joy and gloom alike are contagious.

- Meditate on Nehemiah 8:10, and then write out this verse.

- Reflect on Proverbs 17:22 as well: "A cheerful heart is good medicine, but a crushed spirit dries up the bones." What did King David do when his soul was downcast (see Psalm 42:11 and 43:5)?

Be one who cheers others, not one who dries up the atmosphere. If you can't seem to make your way out of a cloud, go find a Peaceful Phlegmatic who will listen to you or a Popular Sanguine who will bring some sunshine into your day!

- If you are a Perfect Melancholy, do you see the weaknesses in your life, namely, spending too much time planning and being too hard to please? If so, list specific areas in your life (at work, home and so on) where you can loosen up.

- How can being hard to please negatively affect your relationships?

- In most cases, what's more beneficial: to have something done perfectly or to preserve a relationship?

Like the Powerful Choleric, if you are a Perfect Melancholy, you should spend time meditating on verses that warn against judging or being too critical of others, such as Matthew 7:1-2.

Peaceful Phlegmatic

Peaceful Phlegmatics are competent, steady, easygoing and relaxed. They also tend to be excellent listeners. In *Wired That Way,* Marita tells the story of how Ruth, a Peaceful Phlegmatic medical social worker, was able to successfully build a relationship with a difficult patient, Mrs. Jones, a Powerful Choleric. Mrs. Jones was loud and abrupt and had sent away many of the social workers and nurses that had come to visit her. But Ruth was different because, as Mrs. Jones said, "I talk and she listens" (page 70). Being a Peaceful Phlegmatic, Ruth was the perfect social worker for Mrs. Jones simply because she was a good listener.

• From this example of Ruth and Mrs. Jones, what do you learn about the importance of understanding the Personalities?

• What can you learn from Ruth that could help you meet the needs of others and show them that you genuinely care?

• Although Peaceful Phlegmatics and Powerful Cholerics are polar opposites, how does this story show that they can complement each other and work well together?

When you combine the strength of the Peaceful Phlegmatic's ability to listen with a natural bent toward being competent and steady, it quickly becomes evident that the Peaceful Phlegmatic makes a very trustworthy and reliable friend.

• Read the story about Dan on pages 70-72 in *Wired That Way.* What Christlike characteristics does Dan possess?

- Why are these characteristics important for building healthy relationships?

- What does Dan do to stay motivated? What changes has he made to keep from wallowing in his weaknesses and to maximize his strengths?

- How does the Peaceful Phlegmatic's easygoing nature benefit relationships?

- What does Proverbs 14:30 say about this?

On the other hand, the Peaceful Phlegmatic's easygoing nature can lead to a lack of personal drive and ambition. Because Peaceful Phlegmatics are not focused on goals like some of the other Personalities, they can often be perceived as being indifferent, detached and unmotivated.

- In the following passages, what does the apostle Paul relate about the importance of striving for a goal—particularly the goal of reaching others with the gospel?

    1 Corinthians 9:24-27

    Philippians 3:12-14

Jesus' life was also oriented toward a goal. He was decisive. He was determined. He actively pursued His desire and went to the cross to bring us salvation. If you are a Peaceful Phlegmatic, use these verses and these thoughts about Jesus to inspire you to be more decisive and diligent in the things that God has called you to do.

Make a decision to be involved—don't be indifferent to plans. People might assume that you don't care, not only about the activity, but also about them. Remember, your inaction can negatively impact a relationship as much as a negative action can. To fully enjoy and grow your relationships, you must help others believe that you truly care.

Living in Your Strengths

Barbara, a Certified Personality Trainer, is a Popular Sanguine/Powerful Choleric blend. When she heard Marita talk about the difference between living in one's Personality strengths versus living in one's Personality weaknesses, she immediately thought of a man whom she described as the hardest person to work with that she had met in the past 30 years. Barbara writes:

> He was a perfect example of a Powerful Choleric living in his weaknesses. He was bossy, intolerant, wanted instant and unquestioning obedience from everyone, and took credit for everything good that happened within his sphere of influence. If an administrative employee asked any questions about an assignment, his response was always gruff—bordering on insult. He had no patience with anyone—including his fellow managers—who didn't approach him with a servant-like attitude.
>
> This man was an accomplished manipulator who could turn most situations to his advantage. Anyone who crossed him became his enemy and was treated thereafter as a nonperson. More disturbing than just his ignoring this person, this man would then take every opportunity to portray the offending person as incompetent or disloyal to the company. Innocent questions meant to clarify an assignment would be noted in a private computer file and eventually reported as examples of uncooperative behavior.
>
> Several employees had complained to the boss about this man, but no action had been taken because this individual was good at covering his tracks. Eventually he took on the boss—because he believed that he was smarter and should be in that position. Unfortunately for him, he had attempted to

destroy so many people within the organization that when he attempted to discredit the boss, the house of cards collapsed, and he lost his position. There was a huge sigh of relief and a renewed air of excitement and energy in the organization when the staff was told that he was gone!

While similar stories could be told about each Personality type, most of us would not want such a story to be told about us. What would your Personality look like if you were living in your strengths? Consider the following story:

As a woman who spent the majority of her life living in her weaknesses, I am living proof that it is possible for a Popular Sanguine to become organized and productive both at home and on the job. Three years ago, I went on a mission to redeem myself in both my own eyes and the eyes of my family. Today, I am proud to say that not only have I gained the respect of my family, I have also become a positive role model for my children and the true partner that my husband deserves.

Although I considered myself a mature Christian, I now realize I was in major denial about certain areas of my life. Yes, I was disciplined in that I was a faithful wife, devoted mother, didn't drink or smoke, went to church—all the things I thought made me a "good" Christian. However, I was completely undisciplined and reckless in my spending and the running of our household. In fact, out of desperation, my husband hired our Perfect Melancholy daughter to handle our budget and make sure the bills got paid on time! Ordinarily that would have suited me just fine (I would have had even more time to play), except for one problem. You see, I had amassed more than $25,000 in debt, and was juggling several credit cards that my husband wasn't fully aware of. Each month, I was determined to make enough extra to get the debt paid down, and I had convinced myself there was no sense in troubling my hard-working husband with the details of my dilemma.

But my daughter soon figured out how bad things were, and one day I overheard her snitching on me to her dad. I felt like a little kid getting busted by her parents! After initially being incensed by the fact that my husband and daughter were plotting against me behind my back, I then felt a sense of shame wash over me that brought me to my knees. I asked God's forgiveness for being so irresponsible with what He had entrusted to me and then asked my husband's forgiveness for my dishonesty and lack of discipline.

Fortunately, my husband forgave me, and we sat down immediately to devise a plan to get out of debt. It was a humbling experience to watch my credit cards being cut up, but well worth the relief that came with honestly addressing my problems. From there, I set up a budget system that worked well for me, and today I handle all the finances for our home and businesses. Three years ago, no one (least of all me) would have believed that I would be capable of running budgets and working with subcontractors in our property investment business. I have applied that same discipline to keeping my home clean and organized.

I finally learned that if you do the things you ought to do when you ought to do them, you can do the things you want to do when you want to do them. Whereas the Melancholy thrives on all that detail, I now see it as a necessary evil. My Sanguine Personality thrives on the reward at the completion of a job well done. Each time I complete a major goal, I already have a treat planned for myself. *Good girl, Sherri,* I tell myself. *You got the house all clean before bed, so you get to walk to the coffee shop for an hour in the morning.* Or, *You go, girl! You worked on those crummy books for three hours—I think you deserve to have your lunch on the deck and read in your porch swing for an hour.* And my favorite: *Sherri, you're just awesome! You made all those calls today, and worked down at the church, so I think you should grab your camera and your snowshoes and head for the lake!*

This self-talk may seem silly, but to a Sanguine, it makes perfect sense. All those little perks give me the incentive to keep plugging along when all I really want to do is drop everything and go "do lunch" or go shopping. However, the greatest payoff of all is living a life that's pleasing to Christ, receiving the praise of my husband and family, keeping my own self-respect, and enjoying the adventure of each new day as a woman determined to live in her strengths!

—Sherri Villarreal, CPT

Putting It into Practice

Take time to observe people at work, in restaurants, or simply out and about. Do you see anyone with your Personality type behaving in an unattractive manner? If you do, think about how you, too, might need to "dial back the extremes" to avoid being immature or offensive.

- Are you living in your strengths? How so?

- What weaknesses need attention in your life?

- What proactive steps will you take this week to make changes?

Pray the following prayer, asking the Lord to strip you of your weaknesses and give you grace to grow in your strengths.

Lord, I open my heart to You to do Your refining work in me. I pray that my Personality would come into agreement with Your will. Please show me any roots of weaknesses in my life and help me to weed them out. I want to be humble enough to listen to others who might see the weaknesses that I don't see and to make the changes necessary to become a mature, healthy, selfless person.

Please give me the grace to live in my strengths! I want to grow in them, Lord, and to use them to bless You and bless other people. Above all, may my Personality reflect You, Jesus.

In Your name I pray, amen.

CHAPTER 4

PERSONALITY BLENDS

Our Personality blend makes each of us distinct individuals. Like different colors of paint on a painter's palette, our primary and secondary Personalities, when blended together, create a new, totally unique color all our own. Just as mixing blue and red together makes purple and red and yellow together makes orange—two completely different colors—so a Peaceful Phlegmatic/Perfect Melancholy blend might look quite opposite from the Peaceful Phlegmatic/Popular Sanguine blend. Understanding such combinations, and the masks that people can sometimes put over their true Personalities, will help us more fully understand ourselves and our relationships with others.

• Based on your Personality Profile results, or just from what you've read so far, what do you think is your natural personality blend?

• Are you energized more by people or by solitude? Are you focused more on projects or on people?

- In chapter 4 of *Wired That Way*, how did Marita figure out the difference between her husband, Chuck, and her friend Bonnie's husband? How did that reveal Chuck's true personality blend to her?

- What significant difference is there between a Perfect Melancholy/Peaceful Phlegmatic and a Perfect Melancholy/Powerful Choleric?

- What is the significant difference between a Popular Sanguine/Powerful Choleric and Peaceful Phlegmatic/Popular Sanguine?

Natural Combinations

Popular Sanguine/Powerful Choleric

People with the Popular Sanguine/Powerful Choleric blend are the go-getters, full of energy and passion. They thrive on being around people, and they make great leaders. You know when you're around these folks—they exude excitement and a sense of determination. People with this combination tend to take on roles that have them in upfront, people-oriented positions.

- What are some strengths that people with the Popular Sanguine/Powerful Choleric combination possess, and why do you think someone with this Personality mix makes a great leader or spokesperson?

- Is this your Personality combination, or can you think of someone you know who might have this combination? If so, what do you now recognize as being your (or your friend's) greatest strengths? How do you feel you (or your friend) can channel those strengths to make significant progress at work or at home?

In Matthew 11:29, Jesus says, "Take my yoke upon you and learn from me, for I am gentle and humble in heart, and you will find rest for your souls." Note that Jesus mentions *rest* in this verse—something that Popular Sanguine/Powerful Cholerics have a hard time allowing themselves and others to do.

- What can those who have the Popular Sanguine/Powerful Choleric Personality learn from Jesus about holding their strengths and their weaknesses in check?

- In the space provided, write down at least three things that Popular Sanguine/Powerful Cholerics can do to encourage rest in their lives.

Perfect Melancholy/Peaceful Phlegmatic

Proverbs 6:10-11 warns, "A little sleep, a little slumber, a little folding of the hands to rest—and poverty will come on you like a bandit and scarcity like an armed man." Whereas the Popular Sanguine/Powerful Choleric needs to work on getting rest, the Perfect Melancholy/Peaceful Phlegmatic probably needs to work on getting *less* rest. If you're a Perfect Melancholy/Peaceful Phlegmatic, consider Proverbs 6:10-11 and exercise your Perfect Melancholy ability to focus when the Peaceful Phlegmatic in you becomes too laid-back.

- If this is your Personality combination, identify one area or behavior pattern in your life that might be too slow or slothful. If this isn't you, identify such an area or behavior pattern in a person you know who might be Perfect Melancholy/Peaceful Phlegmatic.

- Now write down a simple plan for picking up the pace in that one particular area. (If you are Perfect Melancholy/Peaceful Phlegmatic, tell someone your new resolution so that you have some accountability.)

- Write several words that could describe the strengths of the Perfect Melancholy/Peaceful Phlegmatic:

- What really energizes Perfect Melancholy/Peaceful Phlegmatics? What drains them? What strengths do people with this Personality mix usually possess? Why do others enjoy being around them?

- If this is your Personality combination, how can you tell if you are more Peaceful Phlegmatic or Perfect Melancholy?

- What activity or activities can you involve yourself in to keep from becoming too much of a hermit?

Powerful Choleric/Perfect Melancholy

Marita quotes a Powerful Choleric/Perfect Melancholy named Jean as saying, "I always have to tell myself, 'People are more important than paperwork and goals.'" This is a great example of putting into practice Jesus' greatest commandment to love others as ourselves (see Mark 12:28-31).

This can mean putting aside the projects that might consume too much time and simply carving out time for people. With the Powerful Choleric's emphasis on work and the Perfect Melancholy's need to be alone, the person with this combination has to make a concentrated effort if he or she wants to have a social life.

- If you're a Powerful Choleric/Perfect Melancholy, jot down two or three things you can do to make sure that you keep people a priority in your life:

- What is the major common denominator in this pairing of Personalities?

- What could be the Powerful Choleric/Perfect Melancholy's greatest potential vice?

Another major pitfall that the Powerful Choleric/Perfect Melancholy can easily slip into is that of becoming a workaholic. Despite Jesus' determination to reach a goal and the demands that surrounded Him each day, we see that Jesus frequently took time out to be alone or to get away with His disciples. He went to quiet places where He could slow down and simply pray.

Learning to have balance and set boundaries in regard to work is important—and godly—especially if you have a family. How better to meet the needs of your relatives, your children or your spouse than to spend *time* with them—even just time relaxing at home? While there are seasons in life in which intense, time-consuming focus might be necessary, it's always good to know when to step back and call it a day.

- It's not all warnings and cautions for this Personality combo. These folks are the "worker-bees" of life, as Marita calls them. In the space provided, summarize how this Personality type is praised in the following Proverbs:

Proverbs 12:24

Proverbs 28:19

- Perhaps even the renowned "Proverbs 31 Woman" was a Powerful Choleric/Perfect Melancholy, or maybe a Powerful Choleric/Popular Sanguine? Summarize your thoughts about Proverbs 31 in the space provided.

Cheri shares the following story about her Perfect Melancholy organizational skills versus her Powerful Choleric organizational abilities:

> My mother is a 200 percent Perfect Melancholy. She files her checks in an expanding alphabetical file and organizes the checks by payee. Within each payee group, she then organizes the checks by date. This takes her at least 20 minutes per month, which adds up to 5 hours per year!
>
> When I first got married, my Popular Sanguine nature suggested that I just throw away all cancelled checks, but my Powerful Choleric side knew I needed to keep them. So I got a shoebox and tossed in all checks as they came. When the shoebox filled up, I wrote the approximate years on the side with a black marker, stored it in the garage, and got another empty shoebox. I had the checks organized!
>
> My mother was horrified when she found out I didn't have a "real" system. She tried, in vain, to get me to convert to her system—I gave away all the expanding alphabetical files she brought me and continued with my shoeboxes.
>
> My husband and I had been married about seven years when we bought a house, and the time came to move out of our rental home. I knew we'd paid a hefty security deposit when we moved in, but our landlord had no recollection or record of the deposit. One night, armed with a flashlight, I hunted for the "1991-1993" shoebox in the garage. I brought

it inside, and within 10 minutes, I'd located the cancelled check for our deposit. It saved us $1,500!

That was the one and only time in seven years that I needed to find a check. If I'd used my mother's system, I would have wasted 34 hours and 50 minutes during that time—time that I could have spent accomplishing things!

—Cheri Lynn Gregory, CPT

Peaceful Phlegmatic/Popular Sanguine

Peaceful Phlegmatic/Popular Sanguines are the laid-back, fun-loving ones. They are the life of the party and the ones who give everyone else a feeling of calm and of peace. They usually seem very at ease and comfortable with themselves.

• What can others learn from this particular trait that the Peaceful Phlegmatic/Popular Sanguine possesses?

• Why is the Peaceful Phlegmatic/Popular Sanguine usually "everyone's favorite person"? What are some of the other key strengths that this Personality combination has to offer?

• How can you determine which Personality is the dominant one in this mix?

After his short dissertation on love in 1 Corinthians 13:1-10, the apostle Paul writes, "When I was a child, I talked like a child, I thought like a child, I reasoned like a child. When I became a man, I put childish ways behind me" (v. 11).

- What do you think Paul is saying here, and what can the Peaceful Phlegmatic/Popular Sanguine learn from this advice?

- Write out Ephesians 4:13 and James 1:4 in the space provided.

Striving for Christian maturity is important. Too many young adults never outgrow their desire to be the life of the party—or to have no life, and only party. Their peers pass them by in both work and relational success, and their personal development wanes. Even though some might appear accomplished on the outside, their souls are empty. Considering the strengths of your Personality, how might you come alongside someone like this and help him or her "put childish ways behind"?

Opposing Blends

Marita says that after years of teaching and training on the Personalities, she has yet to meet a person who truly is a *natural* combination of the Popular Sanguine/Perfect Melancholy or Powerful Choleric/Peaceful Phlegmatic. While many people claim to have these Personality blends, it is important to remember that these combinations occur as a result of people *learning* certain behaviors that allow them to function in their environment.

- Do you believe that you have an opposing blend of Personalities, or that one of your friends or relatives has this blend of opposites? If so, which ones?

- After reading through this section in *Wired That Way*, what are some examples of learned behaviors and shared characteristics that might confuse a person as to what his or her real Personality is?

- What might cause some men to think that they are Powerful Cholerics when really they are Peaceful Phlegmatics?

- Think about which of your behaviors are natural and which ones you've learned, and then write those down in the space provided. What role do you think relationships play in this potential Personality confusion?

- Do you personally exhibit any behaviors that don't come naturally because you know they will help you to move ahead personally or professionally?

Masking

Marita tells us, "A mask represents a behavior that people have unconsciously adopted for survival. Usually, this occurs in childhood, often to make their parents happy or to make their parents like them better. The problem with Personality masks, however, is that they create an internal struggle. People may be aware of this internal battle, but since the mask is subconscious, they do not understand the source of the struggle or what to do about it. Ultimately, this causes fatigue, creates stress, and can lead to illnesses" (page 97 in *Wired That Way*).

- What's the difference between a mask and a positive learned behavior?

Marita states that it is "not healthy for people to spend huge amounts of emotional energy trying to be someone whom they are not" (page 97), because people who do this tend to suffer from illnesses as they progress through life. Generally, people who adopt these Personality masks begin to get tired and develop stress-related illnesses around age 40—although they can develop these symptoms sooner. Personality masks are also destructive to a person's self-esteem and interpersonal relationships, as the following story illustrates:

> During my childhood, my all-consuming goal was to be good. My mother proudly says that I never went through a terrible-twos phase; I was always an obedient, eager-to-please child. But during my teens, I became anorexic and bulimic to the point of hospitalization, baffling everyone, including me. I had been such a "good girl," the "perfect child." What had gone wrong? My mother kept asking, "Why are you doing this to me?" and my counselors kept asking, "Why are you doing this to yourself?"
>
> It wasn't until I attended a CLASSeminar as a 24-year-old that I learned the concept of masking and the "a-ha" moments started. As a teenager, I'd taken the Personality Profile and had come out Popular Sanguine/Perfect Melancholy. But now, looking back on my childhood, I realize that the Perfect Melancholy attributes were not real—they weren't "me." They truly made up a mask that I donned to earn what acceptance and approval I could from my mother—a woman one therapist described as "the most perfectionistic and controlling person I've ever met." My mother was such a perfection-as-the-minimum-standard Perfect Melancholy and a my-way-or-the-highway Powerful Choleric that she had little tolerance for my Popular Sanguine nature, and there was no opportunity for my Powerful Choleric side to develop. So I became a rigidly obsessive perfectionist. I over-prepared for all tests, aiming not just for As but 100 percent in everything I did.
>
> Perfectionism is not the only factor that determines whether or not a girl develops an eating disorder, but I have learned that one thing all eating-disorder sufferers have in common is a seriously underdeveloped "sense of self." In my high school journals, on a daily basis I recorded my feelings of being deeply flawed and defective. Now I understand that I was not flawed or defective—I was incomplete! I was missing

half of what makes me who I am—my Powerful Choleric side (which I now refer to affectionately as my better half!).

Although I learned the concept of masking in my early 20s, unhealthy communication patterns had already been firmly laid in my marriage. I married a man much like my mother—a Perfect Melancholy—and had turned all my energies into trying to make him happy. Whenever he became upset with me—as he did during our first week in our new home when I wanted to try putting the couch against one wall but he insisted that it would only look balanced against another wall—I responded with Perfect Melancholy weaknesses: depression, withdrawal and obsessive cleaning. If I'd been living from my Popular Sanguine strengths, I could have lightened the whole situation with humor. If I'd been working in my Powerful Choleric strengths, I could have moved into action on a totally different project. But my only available response was to go into a series of frenzied behaviors that had placated my mother when I was a child, but that did *not* help me *or* my relationship with my husband.

A couple of years later, when our firstborn was a baby, my husband suggested we go to a nearby miniature golf center to have some together time. Elated that my husband wanted to spend time with me, and desperate for some fun, I sprang into action, practically waltzing through the house with joy as I got the diaper bag ready. Unsure whether the stroller or the baby-backpack would be the better choice, I called upstairs to ask which my husband wanted me to pack. I followed his instructions, and soon we were on the road to have some fun!

But just five minutes from the amusement park, everything fell to pieces when my husband asked, "You did remember to pack the backpack, didn't you?" Panicked, I responded, "No, you said to pack the stroller!" Quietly adamant, my husband insisted that he had clearly told me to pack the backpack. I apologized profusely, trying to assure him that I had packed what I heard him tell me to pack. "If we don't have the backpack, we can't go miniature golfing," he declared with finality. Hoping desperately to rescue our much-needed day of fun, I suggested that we go home and quickly make an exchange. "If we go home, I will not leave again," my husband stated, making it clear that I had not just made an error, but a grievous error; my mistake had ruined our day beyond repair.

Once again, my Perfect Melancholy mask was a far more comfortable fit than my undeveloped Powerful Choleric side. I spent the rest of the afternoon crying and berating myself for—once again—making a "little" mistake with such huge consequences. By evening, I'd pulled myself together enough to start trying to redeem myself: I cooked a fabulous dinner; I cleaned the house from top to bottom; I made sure the baby never cried. It took several days, but I ultimately worked my way back into my husband's good graces.

Fifteen years later, I see how unhealthy these interactions were—for me, for my husband, and for our marriage. But at the time, they seemed totally normal. Instinctive. Comfortable. Familiar. Although I no longer had an active eating disorder, the negative effects of wearing the Melancholy mask still impacted my life in so many destructive ways: I actively facilitated a verbally and emotionally abusive relationship; I suffered from frequent headaches and constant neck muscle tension; I fractured a vertebra and ruptured two discs while doing very mild exercise; I developed gallstones at a far-too-early age.

I had learned about the concept of Personality masking when I was in my early 20s, but it took another decade for the consequences of the masking to become so emotionally and physically painful that I absolutely had to change. I've had to drop the Perfect Melancholy mask of pain and perfectionism and develop my true Powerful Choleric self. Obviously, it's not an overnight process. But now I can look back at situations and shake my head in dismay over the frenzied, obsessive way I responded. I now realize that I wasted so much time and energy going around in circles with Perfect Melancholy weaknesses when I could have been moving forward in my Powerful Choleric strengths! I now relate to my mother and husband in much healthier ways. Rather than reacting to them out of my weaknesses, I now consciously translate their words and actions through my understanding of their Personalities so that I respond to their positive intentions with my strengths.

Of course, old habits do die hard. Just a week ago, I discovered that I'd missed out on $200 worth of rebates because I'd done everything right—everything but one specific procedure in small print. I started hyperventilating and getting ready for a good self-beratement session (after all, $200 is a lot of money to lose!) when I stopped myself. I chose not to don the Perfect Melancholy mask. Instead, I tapped into my Popular Sanguine flippancy and thought, *Oh, well!* and my Powerful Choleric arrogance—"Stupid rules!"—and moved on.

Maybe you feel like you are a Popular Sanguine wearing a Perfect Melancholy mask due to pain in your life. This was also true for Lisa. She recently shared the following story with Marita:

As a child, out of necessity, I took on the responsibilities of my younger brother and sister. Single motherhood required my mother to work—sometimes two jobs—to keep a roof over our heads. As the oldest child, I took charge and did my best to care for the house while mom worked. The Powerful Choleric part of my personality thrived.

After I married a Peaceful Phlegmatic/Perfect Melancholy, I continued operating in my "in charge" ways. Just a couple of years into our marriage, I started having stomach pains. It often felt as if someone had punched me in the stomach. I went to a couple of different doctors; they ran every test imaginable and then diagnosed me with Irritable Bowel Syndrome.

It was at about this time that my husband and I were introduced to *The Personality Tree*. After reading the chapter on masking, my husband insisted that I read it. I identified with the concept, and after reading the chapter, I was pretty sure that I was masking. It spurred me to investigate the Personalities more thoroughly. After some time, I found that I am almost equally Powerful Choleric/Popular Sanguine. If you had told me back then that I was even *slightly* Popular Sanguine, I would have laughed myself silly.

While I can tell you that I am now a balanced Powerful Choleric/Popular Sanguine, before the revelation brought by our study of the Personalities, I had so skillfully masked the Popular Sanguine side that even I didn't know who I was. Now, I rarely have that pain in my stomach, but when I do, I quickly look to my level of stress and how authentically I am living my life.

Can you relate to Lisa's story? As Marita mentions in *Wired That Way*, if you can, you need to ask yourself, *When did the fun stop?*

- If you think you are a Peaceful Phlegmatic/Powerful Choleric, take the same inventory. What circumstances in your life might have caused you to take on a mask?

- What healthy steps can you take to embrace who you really are?

Perhaps you feel that you are a Powerful Choleric wearing a Perfect Melancholy mask because your natural drive to lead has been suppressed in your life. Consider this final story of how this occurred in Kathryn's life:

> Kathryn is a Powerful Choleric/Popular Sanguine. When she was first introduced to the Personalities, she took the Personality Profile and shared the material with her mother—also a Powerful Choleric. As Kathryn explained to her mother that she was a Powerful Choleric/Popular Sanguine, her mother said, "You are not Powerful Choleric—I'd bet my life savings that you are Peaceful Phlegmatic. When you were a child, I could not get you to do anything!"
>
> Looking back, Kathryn now understands that with a Powerful Choleric mother, she subconsciously realized that there was only room for one chief. Because Kathryn was the child, it wasn't going to be her; and since she couldn't win, she tuned out. Her mother encouraged her to be the cute Popular Sanguine, but her true Powerful Choleric Personality was squished.
>
> By the time Kathryn entered school, the repressed Powerful Choleric traits were seeping out in wrong ways. Even at that young age, she talked with a bite in her tone. It wasn't that there was something that she was mad at specifically, she was just generally angry at the world—there was a rage growing inside her.

In her adult life, Kathryn's Peaceful Phlegmatic mask was also encouraged. She married into a strict religious family and was told that she needed to be docile and quiet. Her internal rage increased and began to spill out more and more frequently in cutting sarcastic remarks. She frequently quipped, "Only fools or brave people hang out with me." Her caustic behaviors caused her to get kicked out of several churches and alienate would-be friends.

Once Kathryn learned about the Personalities and could see who she really was, she was able to embrace her Powerful Choleric Personality and begin to cultivate its healthy side. Huge changes have taken place in her life. Once she began to live in her Powerful Choleric strengths, she and her mother were able to interact more as peers instead of competitors. Because Powerful Cholerics respect strength, her mother now has a new respect for her, and Kathryn has learned to draw strength from practicing self-control rather than the raw power of rage.

Can you relate to Kathryn's story? If so, you need to ask yourself if you have bought into the Powerful Choleric's unwritten rule: "If I can't win, I won't play the game."

- If you think this is true in your life, what circumstances might have caused you to take on a mask?

- Marita states that if Powerful Cholerics do put on a mask, "it is usually as a result of something in their lives being out of control." Is there anything in your life that feels completely out of control?

If you recognize that a masking has taken place in your life or in the life of someone you love, take some time to think and write about what you perceive. Pray and ask God to help you remedy the situation. Finding someone else with whom you can talk and pray over the situation can be helpful too. Then, once you can identify what has happened to create the mask, take the appropriate steps to begin walking in your strengths and/or helping your child, spouse or friend to begin walking in his or hers.

Meanwhile, remember to keep the good traits that you acquired by masking. And don't panic, perhaps you're not masking at all. Perhaps you've grown into a mature individual who is reflecting more and more strengths from each of the four Personalities. That's a good thing! Becoming more like Christ means growing in those positive attributes that weren't naturally yours to begin with.

As Ephesians says, we are to "become mature, attaining to the whole measure of the fullness of Christ" (4:13), and "speaking the truth in love, we will in all things grow up into him who is the Head, that is, Christ. From him the whole body, joined and held together by every supporting ligament, grows and builds itself up in love, as each part does its work" (v. 15-16).

Putting It into Practice

After reading the various stories of individuals who began masking as children in response to their parents' behavior, examine your relationship with your own children (if you have them) or your relationship with your parents, close relatives or spouse.

- Do you see how masking might be happening or might have happened?

- Do you see any instances in which one person's weaknesses overpowered another, or one person masked his or her true personality in an attempt to gain acceptance from another?

- Write down one way in which you will intentionally let someone close to you know how much you appreciate the strengths you see in him or her. Remember to keep his or her tastes in mind too. How might such a compliment be best received?

If you feel like you're trying to "keep beach balls under water" because you're juggling two opposing Personalities, or if you feel some of the symptoms of masking, stop here and pray this prayer:

Father, Your Word says that You "created my inmost being" and that You saw my "unformed body" (see Psalm 139:13,16). You are the one who wired me as I am. I ask You, then, to reveal my God-given Personality combination to me. If I've masked or hidden the true me, please show me. If I've formed unhealthy patterns to cope with or please other people, please reveal that to me too and heal me from this.

I trust You, Lord, to help me become my true self and to make the most of all You have created me to be and do. Amen.

CHAPTER 5

EMOTIONAL NEEDS

Ever wondered why your spouse or parent or boss seemed so insensitive? Why, when you needed them to hug you or to listen to you (without giving advice), they were totally oblivious to you and did exactly the opposite of what you wanted? Have you ever felt that when you were trying to "treat others as you'd want to be treated," your efforts were going unappreciated?

Most likely, you were wrestling with *emotional needs*—those core necessities that our Personalities depend on for emotional well-being. As Marita says, these needs are not wants or desires, but are hardwired into who we are. "When these emotional needs are not met in the proper way, we are more likely to do whatever it takes to ease the pain or craving that occurs because of these unfulfilled needs" (page 127 in *Wired That Way*).

Remember, the goal of understanding our Personalities (and much of the Christian life) is to improve our relationships with others and with God. God calls us to love other people as Christ would love them.

- Who do you wish to have a better relationship with? It could be a parent, a child, employee or spouse, someone at your church or a long-time friend. Write their names here:

- Based on what you understand about the Personalities, what do you believe to be these individuals' primary and secondary Personalities?

Each Personality has a set of core needs that is different from the others. This presents a challenge when we try to meet the needs of others and want them to meet our own needs. However, with a clear understanding of what makes others tick, and with a willingness to communicate with them accordingly, we can see significant improvements in a short time.

What Do Popular Sanguines Need?

While having an emotional need for attention is normal for a Popular Sanguine, clamoring for praise and continually putting the spotlight on one's self is not only unhealthy but also ungodly.

- What would be an example of getting godly attention?

- Think of the Popular Sanguines in your life. List a few specific, simple and healthy things that you can do to meet their need for attention:

- Marita writes about a young woman named Nikki who sought to have her need for affection met through sexual relationships with several men. Have you (or has anyone you know) struggled with such behavior in an attempt to meet core needs for affection?

- If so, and if you (or the person you know) haven't yet dealt with that problem, stop now and ask the Lord to deliver you from this lifestyle choice. If you wish, use the space below to write out your prayer.

In Ephesians 1:6, Paul says that God has "accepted" us in Christ (*KJV*). And just prior to this verse in Ephesians 1:4, Paul says that God "chose us"—we didn't have to do anything to gain His acceptance!

- Write out Ephesians 1:4-8 in the space provided.

- What can Popular Sanguines learn from these verses about God's acceptance of them?

What Do Powerful Cholerics Need?

In the book of Nehemiah, God called Nehemiah into a place of leadership for rebuilding the wall of Jerusalem. Nehemiah faced attack and persecution on all sides, yet he persevered and he completed the job.

- Skim through the following passages in Nehemiah and jot down ideas about the essential leadership characteristics that Nehemiah demonstrated as he carried out this enormous task.

Nehemiah 1:4-10

Nehemiah 2:3-9

Nehemiah 4:6-23

Nehemiah 5:13-19

Nehemiah 6:15-16

Nehemiah 7:1-3

Nehemiah 13:7-14

- In these passages, what about Nehemiah seems to indicate a Powerful Choleric Personality? What can Powerful Cholerics learn from Nehemiah in terms of maximizing their strengths and communicating their needs (even to God)?

Consider Marita's advice: "Depending on the level of maturity, Powerful Cholerics may attack, sever relationships, or extend grace. Immature Powerful Cholerics (those living in their weaknesses) who are betrayed will attack so-called team members or friends and attempt to destroy them. The knee-jerk reaction of most Powerful Cholerics is to go home—thinking it is the other person's loss. For high functioning Powerful Cholerics (those living in their strengths), when faced with a situation in which they feel betrayed, they will try to see the other's point of view—realizing that very few people are really out to get them. These Powerful Cholerics will offer grace and resolution" (page 112).

- In the space provided, summarize what Ephesians 4:31-32 says about extending grace to others.

- Write out Luke 6:36-37 in the space provided. In light of this passage, what might Jesus say to a Powerful Choleric who wanted to lash out at someone who had failed to meet his or her needs?

- If you're in a relationship with a Powerful Choleric, what kind of action can you take to show your support of that person and to meet his or her emotional needs?

Everyone—even Powerful Cholerics—must acknowledge and submit to God's ultimate control, His sovereignty. Only by cultivating an obedient, trusting relationship with God and by learning healthy submission to those in authority will Powerful Cholerics be able to truly walk in strength as the leader God intended them to be.

- What does Matthew 8:5-9 indicate about the importance of submitting to authority, even though you might be in a position of authority yourself?

- Write down the name of one Powerful Choleric whom you can praise this week for the work that person has done or a project he or she has recently completed. Briefly state what you might say to that person.

If you are a Powerful Choleric, consider those whom you work or live with who haven't finished their projects. How can you praise them for *their* achievements? Though they might not measure up to your personal standards of excellence, remember that other Personality types need praise and approval as well. And by hearing praise from a Powerful Choleric, others might just feel encouraged enough to raise the bar on their own work!

What Do Perfect Melancholies Need?

Consider Marita's story about how she responded to her husband's emotional needs when his employer transferred him from one work facility to another. Her temptation was to cheer him up and help him feel as excited as she was about all the potential in the new move.

- What was Chuck's response to Marita when she asked, "What do you need from me right now?"

- Have you ever had a similar experience with a Perfect Melancholy? What was the outcome of the conversation? Did the "other Personality" try to cheer up the Perfect Melancholy, or did he or she wait to hear and understand the Perfect Melancholy's feelings?

- If the situation didn't end as well as Chuck and Marita's, what could you do or say differently next time to encourage results that would meet the Perfect Melancholy's needs? If the end result was positive, what were the ingredients of the conversation that led to a happy ending?

- In the space provided, write out James 1:19. How does this apply to meeting the needs of a Perfect Melancholy?

- In *Wired That Way*, we read about what Andrea did for her Perfect Melancholy husband to meet his emotional need for space. If you have a Perfect Melancholy spouse, child or roommate, list a few things you might be able to do to offer him or her space in your home environment.

- What practical thing(s) can you do to meet that person's need for silence without making everyone else in the house feel like they're living in a monastery?

What Do Peaceful Phlegmatics Need?

Consider what Marita states about the Peaceful Phlegmatic child: "This child is likely to grow up to be the person who has fallen through the cracks her entire life. For this type of child, her parents will need to instill in her a sense of self-worth—otherwise she may fail to receive this in her life. She will need to feel like her parents value her, not for what she does or for what she produces, but simply because of who she is."

- Who in your life fits this description? How can you show that person how valuable he or she is simply because of who he or she is?

Nowhere else do we find a clearer message of our self-worth than in the Bible. First and foremost, this is seen in Jesus' suffering and death on our behalf—on your behalf—because our lives have immeasurable worth in His eyes!

- Look up the following passages of Scripture and summarize each one in the space provided. What does each passage tell you about your worth to God?

Psalm 18

Psalm 139

Isaiah 49:16

• Do Peaceful Phlegmatics feel more respected when praised for what they do or when they are cherished for who they are? Why do you think this is?

Although Peaceful Phlegmatics need to have a feeling of self-worth and obtain respect from others, being placed in the spotlight isn't usually what they had in mind. Be sensitive when honoring them, doing it in such a way that considers their needs and feelings—not your own.

• If you're a Peaceful Phlegmatic, write down how you will communicate your needs to those closest to you the next time you're feeling deprived. Remember, often other Personalities want to be sensitive (especially if they've studied the Personalities), but they can't read your mind!

• And for the other Personalities, take Marita's admonition to heart: "Listen to the Peaceful Phlegmatics in your life. What have they been quietly asking you to do? Make it a priority." Write down a few ways you can respect or honor the Peaceful Phlegmatic in your life.

Leading a More Fulfilled Life

Again, the goal of trying to understand yourself and the people around you is to have better, healthy, life-giving relationships! The charts provided in *Wired That Way* will help you to quickly identify and meet the needs of others. Of course, this will take practice and patience, so don't feel discouraged if you're not a Personality expert just yet. Just making an effort to put others' needs before your own and to understand that their needs might be different from yours will have a huge impact on your relationships.

- Recall Marita's story about Marilyn and her daughter, Meredith. What does this story reveal about how crucial it is to consider Personality differences before jumping to conclusions about your child (or your spouse, your employee, your pastor, and so on)?

- Do you need to follow Marilyn's example by asking forgiveness from people in your life for having misjudged them and having tried to make them more like yourself?

Understanding our own and others' emotional needs will lay the foundation for a happier, healthier, more fulfilled life. Once we grasp how we're wired, we can take the necessary steps to control our own emotional health and to help others with theirs. When we recognize the unhealthy ways in which we've tried to meet those needs, we can repent and move on. We can work toward managing our emotional well-being in the ways that God intended.

This is especially true when we face the loss of a loved one in our life. Georgia Shaffer, MA, a Certified Personality Trainer, writes the following regarding depression and the Personalities:

> As the level of stress in our society continues to climb, so does the number of people who are depressed. Although there are many causes of depression, any unwanted change can trigger feelings of sadness—especially when we think there is no hope that our life will improve in the future.
>
> None of the Personalities is immune to depression when confronted with a significant loss. However, our individual response to adversity is often an extension of our basic Personality and impacts our style of coping. Popular Sanguines become depressed when life is no longer fun or they feel isolated or disconnected from others. In contrast, Perfect Melancholies become depressed when life is far from perfect and they see no hope of organizing or improving the situation. Powerful Cholerics are depressed when life is out of

control. They will try their best to fix the situation or gain the upper hand until they realize there is nothing they can do. And troubling times bring too many problems for the Peaceful Phlegmatics. Rather than getting the peace and quiet they love, they suddenly are thrown into a life of conflict and chaos that leads them to deep sadness.

Popular Sanguines

Of the four Personalities, the Popular Sanguine often has the toughest time not only being in the hospital but also having to visit someone there. They do not like going to a funeral or caring for someone over an extended period of time. Let's face it, these experiences aren't anything close to fun or exciting.

Becky, a Popular Sanguine who had a bone marrow transplant several months before I did, brightly told me of all the people who visited and the gifts she received when she arrived home from the hospital. But then her voice dropped, and she looked down at the floor. "That was three months ago," she said quietly. "Now I think everyone has forgotten about me." She was no longer receiving the attention, affection and approval that she so desperately needed.

To make matters worse, she and her husband had borrowed more than $60,000 to pay for their portion of the transplant not covered by insurance. Their tight budget allowed only for the necessities. Becky couldn't go shopping for new clothes or go out to eat, which were two activities she had always enjoyed. Fortunately, a group of caring friends recognized Becky's predicament. Twice a month they took her to lunch at different restaurants in town. Becky looked forward to these excursions.

But what if you are a Popular Sanguine and don't have the support of any close friends, as Becky did? Begin by writing down a list of activities that you enjoy (if you haven't had fun for a long time, this may be a difficult assignment). Give yourself time to think. What brings you a sense of relief and distracts you from the mundane chores in your life? Maybe you enjoy riding a horse, eating an ice-cream cone or going to a movie. Next, make a conscious effort to carve out the space and time needed to put some pleasure in the midst of your difficulties. Each day, try to do *something* to put a hint of joy into your life.

Perfect Melancholy

The Perfect Melancholy takes life seriously and is the most prone to depression. They know the depths of despair. As I mentioned, they become depressed when life is not perfect and there appears to be no way to straighten things out. Those who are Perfect Melancholies need sensitivity to their feelings as well as silence and space to think. A sense of warmth and caring is very important for their sensitive spirit. Don't tell them to lighten up!

Those with the Perfect Melancholy Personality also treasure silence and space. When Missy's husband was killed in an automobile accident, she desperately needed time to be alone and work through her feelings of anger and sadness. Legal concerns and responsibilities for the house and family left Missy feeling overwhelmed. She confided to a friend, "I desperately want some silence. Time to think! But it doesn't exist at this house. The girls either have the TV on, the music blaring or are fighting about the telephone." Her friend offered to stay with the girls for a weekend. This gave Missy the much-needed opportunity to get away by herself.

As a Perfect Melancholy, what can you do for yourself? Humor or a lighthearted approach to life is not a Perfect Melancholy strength. If you can provide opportunity for some laughter, it may help to relieve the stress. Realize that you need solitude to recharge your physical, mental and emotional resources that have been depleted by loss. Be willing to create or schedule time to be alone. Not just a few minutes, but blocks of time to read, write and go deep within. Maybe, like Missy, you can get the chance to go away for a few days. Quite often, when we are able to get away physically, we get a fresh perspective on our situation as well as a chance to rest and renew.

Because Perfect Melancholies love organization and perfection, any little deed or action that will help them move in that direction will be appreciated. When my cancer treatments lasted for a year and a half, my desk and drawers were no longer organized. Finding simple things like the stapler became next to impossible. Although I didn't have the strength to rearrange things, I did not lose my desire to have them in order. As the months went on, I got more and more depressed searching for things in the midst of the accumulating clutter.

A close friend volunteered to help me get the house back in order. About once a week, we spent an hour or two cleaning a closet or a few drawers. It was a slow process, but I felt better knowing that some progress was being made. And gradually my house was cleaned and reorganized!

Powerful Choleric

Of the four Personalities, when dealing with a major tragedy the Powerful Choleric will have the most difficulty. They want to be powerful, not weak and helpless.

A Powerful Choleric friend who was diagnosed with cancer once told me, "I felt fine. I didn't think anything was wrong with me. I went for a routine checkup and found out that I had cancer. I felt like my body had betrayed me." She was angry, which can be one of the easiest emotions for Powerful Cholerics to express.

Shortly after John lost his business, he said, "I'm a stable, logical person—not crazy. Why do I feel like I'm losing it—falling apart?" Maybe because he is losing it—"it" being control. And Powerful Cholerics hate that feeling.

Powerful Cholerics appreciate when others recognize the challenge or difficulty of the crisis they're facing. A simple statement like "I don't know how you manage, considering all you are facing" means a lot to the Powerful Choleric during stressful times. Unfortunately, in tough times, they may not have the ability to achieve and accomplish, to "do something." For a week during my bone marrow transplant, I had an infection and a fever of 104 degrees. My main accomplishment of the day was a walk around my tiny hospital room supporting myself on an IV pole filled with bags of drugs. I felt worthless.

One day when I felt especially useless, I received a letter from my college roommate's daughter. Kiera was 13 years old when she wrote:

Dear Georgia,

I'm writing this letter to let you know about a speech I did in school. It was to be about the person we admire most. I picked you as that person. After class my classmates came up to me and told me how brave and determined they thought you are. I admire your sense of will and strength. You're an astounding woman, and I give you my very best.

Kiera

I was stunned. I thought she must have the wrong person! The idea that I could be valued just for who I was, rather that what I had accomplished, was so foreign to me.

As a Powerful Choleric, what can you do for yourself when you are depressed? Find areas where you can be proactive. Even if it is deciding what you will eat for dinner or which movie to rent, the ability to choose will empower you and help to restore some sense of control.

If you have the physical ability, working harder, exercising longer or starting a new project will help to lift your depression. Powerful Cholerics like to get their difficulties behind them. Wallowing in despair is not their style. However, remember that caring, healthy relationships can be the best medicine for depression. Be sure to balance work and exercise with time with your loved ones.

Peaceful Phlegmatic
The Peaceful Phlegmatic can be depressed when life is filled with problems and conflicts that can't be ignored. They tend to share very little, and they have the tendency to stuff their emotions inside them. Unfortunately, they expend a tremendous amount of energy when they internalize their feelings, which only adds to their depression and further depletes their energy.

For weeks after the death of Michael's wife, several women in his church provided meals, cleaned his house and fussed over his every need. "I got worn out just listening to them," Michael said. As a Peaceful Phlegmatic, he was unable to tell the women what he really desired: "some peace and quiet." Instead, he spaced out in front of the TV set and took frequent naps.

What can you do for yourself if you are a Peaceful Phlegmatic? Allow yourself a chance to rest and to do something you enjoy. Maybe that is fishing, golfing, hiking, reading or watching TV. Remember that being around people 24 hours a day will be draining to you.

Although grieving a loss or shattered dream is painful, it's so much healthier when you acknowledge that it does hurt. Please understand that the most toxic emotions are those we ignore or stuff inside. They are toxic to our relationships and poisonous to our health, as they will literally eat us alive on the inside.

Even though as a Peaceful Phlegmatic you will prefer to avoid conflict or problems at all costs, by journaling or talking to a safe person like a close friend, pastor or counselor, you will rid yourself of those potentially destructive feelings.

Understanding that each Personality copes with loss and depression differently will allow you to avoid many misunderstandings. Much tension can be alleviated when you allow the people in your life to grieve in their own way. There is a saying that the grass is always greener on the other side of the fence. I found the grass is usually greener where it is given what it needs—be it sunlight, water, lime or nitrogen.

What do you or the people in your life desire? An opportunity for excitement in the midst of pain? A chance to withdraw and sort things out? Time to work or exercise harder? Or moments to pull away from the realities of life to quietly rest? Providing for these needs during difficult times can be the difference between continuing to hurt and beginning to heal.

—Georgia Shaffer, MA, CPT

Putting It into Practice

Every human being is born into the world with a fallen nature. We have a natural inclination to do things, no matter how subtle, that are destructive to ourselves, to others and, above all, to our relationship with God. Every person who has ever walked the planet—with the exception of Jesus—has sought to meet his or her needs and desires in harmful ways. This is (or often leads to) sin. Being overly busy or overly talkative isn't necessarily sinful behavior, but it can be an attempt (sometimes subconsciously) to meet emotional needs in an unhealthy and selfish way.

The only remedy for having our deepest needs met—for forgiveness, eternal life and an enduring sense of self-worth—is Jesus Christ. Only His death and resurrection can bring us into new life. From that foundation, we can build happy, successful, righteous, unselfish lives that will draw others to God and to the same healing and transformation that we've found.

- Write out 1 Corinthians 3:10-11 in the space provided. What does this passage tell you about every solution to meeting our needs outside of Jesus?

- On an index card or a separate piece of paper, write out Philippians 2:4. Put this verse somewhere where you'll see it every day (your bathroom mirror, refrigerator, desk at work). Memorize it. Make it a priority each day to put this biblical principle into practice as you consider the Personalities and the emotional needs of the people with whom you live and work.

CHAPTER 6

MARRIAGE

Opposites attract, but, as Marita writes, "Without an understanding of our Personalities and how we can complement each other, we switch from 'attract' mode to 'attack' mode!" (page 134 in *Wired That Way*). Every relationship takes work! Because of this, we need to be equipped with the proper tools for building a strong, healthy and loving marriage.

As we discussed earlier, the foundation for any great growth and any great relationship must be Christ. The same holds true with marriage— real growth and change can only happen when there is a commitment to Jesus at the core of the relationship. Next comes your commitment to understanding yourself and your spouse and how your Personalities work together.

- If you are married, what are your spouse's primary and secondary Personalities? According to Marita, what is the advantage of marrying someone who is your opposite?

- Have you ever had an experience with your significant other (or someone close to you) that resulted in disappointment because your expectations weren't met? How did you feel when you realized things weren't turning out the way you had hoped?

- What did you do in response to your significant other (or other person close to you)? What was his or her response? How did the situation end?

A Segment for Singles

If you're single, it's unwise to assume that love alone will be all you need to get you through marriage (it might get you through the honeymoon!). Proverbs 11:14 says, "Where there is no guidance the people fall, but in abundance of counselors there is victory" (*NASB*). For a strong marriage, study the Personalities and seek out godly counsel. Often the observations of others outside our relationship can help us to see differences, flaws and red flags that we might not otherwise notice in a potential spouse.

- If you're single, what have you learned from previous relationships or from observing the marriages of others?

- The apostle Paul probably knew a little more about Personalities in his day than we might give him credit for. Read 1 Corinthians 7, and then write down a quick summary of what Paul says about remaining single. Does Paul approve of singleness?

- What is a wise Personality combination for marriage relationships, and what's good to have in common with your prospective spouse? If you're dating or engaged, have you taken the time to discover and discuss your Personality similarities and differences?

If you are single, you need to be intentional about doing single "well." Georgia Shaffer, MA, writes the following about the importance of just being yourself and not trying to put on a false Personality to impress prospective mates:

Because I've been divorced and single for 15 years, as a professional speaker I'm often asked to speak at singles' conferences. One of the things I've come to realize is that very few singles are intentional about doing single well. One of the reasons I think singles "let life happen" or react to life is because, like me, their intention was never to be single for any length of time.

The thought never even crossed my mind that I needed to be intentional about doing single well. And I can tell you that when I did make that choice to cultivate a healthy lifestyle, I discovered very few of us can articulate or have a clear concept of what a healthy Christian single looks like in today's culture—it's not what was portrayed on the TV shows *Sex and the City* or *Friends*.

I have found that singleness is a life skill that most of us will need during one season or another, but which few of us have been taught. Whether we are single by design, divorce or death, we need to create healthy habits for love and life. One of those habits I focus on during a weekend conference is cultivating caring relationships. All too often, some singles focus all of their energy on dating.

Even if we have someone even "marginally" in our life, we pour an enormous amount of time and attention into that relationship, while ignoring our other relationships. We lower our standards just so that we have someone in our life. We may tolerate relationships that are not safe or not God's best for us. We either aren't aware of our God-given Personality, or we pretend to be someone we're not.

However, unless we learn how to cultivate significant relationships with Christ and others, in the single season of our lives, we won't suddenly possess this ability just because we get married.

I encourage singles to use the Personalities to understand who God created them to be and to have the courage to just be themselves. One single man recently said to me, "I'm tired of going out with women who pretend they are fun and easygoing, like a Popular Sanguine/Peaceful Phlegmatic, and then six months later they become a career-focused Perfect Melancholy/Powerful Choleric. Or maybe they pretend they are a Powerful Choleric and end up being the Peaceful Phlegmatic. Why can't they communicate honestly from the beginning who they really are?"

This man understood that the foundation of intimacy is honesty. He understood that each Personality has wonderful strengths they bring into a relationship, but when the women do the "bait and switch" routine, he loses interest and respect.

If you are single and desire to be married someday, don't focus on the romantic "in love" feeling as *the* ultimate. Using your understanding of the Personalities, create your own community and family that will meet your need for connection and companionship. Rather than struggle with those feelings of loneliness, develop a network of people whom you encourage and support and who, in turn, care for you.

—Georgia Shaffer, MA, CPT

One Square in Common

In *Wired That Way*, Marita states, "I have found that the marriages that take the least amount of work are those that have what I call one square in common" (pages 136-137). Although people are naturally attracted to those who have an opposite Personality from their own, marriages in which each partner shares at least one common Personality type are typically easier for those involved.

- If you're married (or approaching marriage), do you have a common square with your (prospective) spouse? If so, which one? How does this common square benefit your relationship?

- What activities can you enjoy together within your shared square of interests? Have you had to learn to do anything on your own that, when you first got married, you had hoped to share with your spouse?

Perhaps you've given up certain things you enjoy, not because your husband or wife doesn't want you to do them, but because he or she doesn't want to do them with you. While togetherness is a goal, it's also good to keep your emotional needs in mind and not let go of every activity you used to love. Your spouse may not be wired that way, but you are! So if your spouse doesn't mind your getting out there (or staying in) and doing whatever it is you enjoy doing, do it!

In the story "Reconcilable Differences" in *Wired That Way*, when Sherri had an epiphany that both she and her husband were "unique creations of God," she began to appreciate that each of them had been actually wired by God—it was no accident. Together with the Lord and with their newfound understanding of the Personalities, they salvaged their marriage, which has since become a dynamic, life-giving relationship.

What if they had divorced? Think of all the lives that would not have been changed through them (as they now share their story and the example of their love with others), and of all the joy and growth they would have missed out on. Divorce is not the answer!

Opposites Attract?

Even if you are married to your polar opposite (Popular Sanguine/Powerful Choleric to Perfect Melancholy/Peaceful Phlegmatic), your marriage can work and can be peaceful and *enjoyable*. One way to make it so is by serving your husband or wife. This can be through deliberate actions or by simply being sensitive to what he or she needs on a regular basis. This is what being Christlike is all about.

- Read Matthew 20:28. What wisdom can you extract from this in regard to your marriage?

- Remember Romans 12:18, the verse Marita began the book with: "If it is possible, as far as it depends on you, live at peace with everyone"? What are you doing currently to "live at peace" with your spouse?

It's not only *peace* that we're striving for, but also to have strong, dynamic marriages that point the world to Jesus. As Sherri wrote, "We are living proof that God knew just what He was doing when He allowed opposites to attract—He intended for people to complement each other's strengths and compensate for one another's weaknesses. The possibilities are truly limitless when we make the decision that settling for mediocrity in our relationships, or in our life, is no longer an option" (page 144).

- What are some expectations and/or goals that you have for your marriage? Have you shared these with your spouse?

- Do you know what your spouse desires for your marriage? Do you share the same goals or are your goals different?

- If you're married to someone with a Personality distinctly different from your own, has he or she ever surprised you with a special gift or an activity that typically only you enjoy? If so (and especially if he or she is a Powerful Choleric), have you praised him or her for a job well done?

- List a few ideas for gifts that you can give or activities that you can plan (that you might not even particularly enjoy) to bless your spouse—activities that will show him or her how much you enjoy spending time with him or her and value the person God has created him or her to be.

As Sherri says, "The possibilities are truly limitless." Take the time today to find out how you and your spouse can use your Personality strengths and differences to make a difference in the world—and in your own lives!

Emotional Needs in Marriage

Meeting another person's emotional needs takes some effort. You almost have to get into the other person's head—into his or her skin—to understand what works. While literally getting in there isn't possible, grasping your spouse's Personality is possible! Once you know your spouse's Personality, you will then have some good ideas about what emotional needs he or she has as well.

- What is wrong with simply doing for our spouse what we would like done for us (in other words, meeting his or her emotional needs the way we want ours to be met)?

- What is required before you can begin to meet the needs of your spouse in the best possible way?

- In the story "Engaged by a Spreadsheet" in *Wired That Way* (see pages 147-149), how was Mike trying to show his love for Wendy? What would have really melted her heart?

Popular Sanguine/Perfect Melancholy

Popular Sanguines crave attention and approval, while Perfect Melancholies seek perfection. Because of this, in a marriage between a Popular Sanguine and a Perfect Melancholy, the Popular Sanguine spouse will never be "perfect" enough to appease his or her Perfect Melancholy mate. As Marita states, "Of course, they can never be perfect enough for the Perfect Melancholy to praise them—the Perfect Melancholies will feel that if they offer the praise the Popular Sanguines need, the Popular Sanguines might think that what they did was good enough, when it could have been better" (page146).

- If you are the spouse of a Popular Sanguine, what can you do today to meet your spouse's need for attention and approval?

- In what practical ways can you show your spouse that you love and appreciate him or her for who he or she is—imperfections and all?

Marita states, "Perfect Melancholies need their Popular Sanguine spouse to hurt when they hurt and cry when they cry. They also need time to themselves. Perfect Melancholies recharge their batteries with solitude" (page 149).

- Are you the spouse of a Perfect Melancholy? If so, what can you start doing today to better meet your spouse's need for empathy and time alone?

- What does it mean to "play the silence" (as Marita describes it in *Wired That Way*) for a Perfect Melancholy?

- In the space provided, write out Proverbs 20:5. How can this verse be applied to the Popular Sanguine/Perfect Melancholy marriage?

If the emotional needs of Popular Sanguines are unmet in their marriage, they may attempt to get the attention and affection that they desire from other places. Some Popular Sanguines may go to further extremes by changing jobs or even having an affair. Krista found this to be true in her marriage. While she did not actually have an affair, she realized how close she came to having one when her marriage was at its lowest point. This is her story:

> During the worst part of our marriage—when my husband and I had both finally realized we weren't going to get what we needed from each other—I realized that I was receiving an unusual amount of unexpected attention from Todd, the husband of a friend. My friend was furious with him because Todd had lost his job and wasn't getting a new one. She was giving him the cold shoulder in all areas of their marriage.
>
> At first, I noticed that Todd hugged me just a little longer than was normal for our social relationship. It felt good, and I chose to encourage, rather than discourage, these hugs. Then I realized that Todd was hanging around me a lot more. At every gathering that we attended with our spouses, Todd would bring me food and drinks. It felt good to receive so much male attention, so I charmingly smiled and thanked him rather than rebuffing his attentions. (I told myself that I was modeling "positive male ego building" for my friend.) Then I caught myself having a witty banter with Todd about sex—something I had never discussed with a male other than my own husband. It felt good, fun, daring and provocative.
>
> I felt more alive around Todd than I'd felt in a long time around my own husband. One evening, as Todd was laughing way too hard at something I'd said that wasn't particularly funny, it suddenly occurred to me that if I were to just say the word, he would make a hotel reservation for us. Although this realization gave me a special thrill, it also scared me. Like the puppy who chases a car but wouldn't know what to with it when she caught it, I realized that I was about to be in over my head.

Powerful Choleric/Peaceful Phlegmatic

Powerful Cholerics have a need to accomplish tasks for their own self-worth, and they need to receive praise for their efforts. Powerful Cholerics set lofty goals for their daily productivity and will only rest when they have accomplished everything on their to-do list. Because Powerful Cholerics respect production and achievement, a Peaceful Phlegmatic spouse will never accomplish enough to gain the respect of their Powerful Choleric mate. As Marita states, in the Powerful Choleric's mind, "Even if that 'do nothing' spouse suddenly got active today, he or she could never make up for years of having lived on the sidelines" (page 153).

• In what ways are the Powerful Choleric and the Peaceful Phlegmatic fundamentally different?

• What is one of the best things a husband or wife could ever say to his or her Powerful Choleric mate? Why is it not wise to withhold appreciation from a Powerful Choleric?

• Are you married to a Powerful Choleric? List a few of his or her recent projects or achievements.

• Even God recognizes our genuine need for praise (see Proverbs 27:2). Be sure to let your spouse know that you appreciate all that he or she does around the house and elsewhere!

- Now, how can the Powerful Choleric best encourage the Peaceful Phlegmatic spouse? What physical action should Powerful Cholerics take to show their Peaceful Phlegmatic spouse that they are serious about meeting that spouse's emotional needs?

- What sometimes causes Peaceful Phlegmatics to cease communicating?

- Write out Ephesians 4:2. How can Powerful Cholerics employ the message of this verse in their marriages?

- What does Marita mean when she says that Powerful Cholerics need to "think Japanese" in terms of their Peaceful Phlegmatic spouse?

Putting It into Practice

When knowledge, wisdom and understanding are put into practice, things change. Prayer changes things as well. Prayer can change a marriage—and it can change *you*! The power of God can change people and even circumstances that may seem completely hopeless. He will honor your prayers of faith.

- Look up James 5:13-16. What do these verses say about the power of prayer and faith?

Taking the time to pray for your marriage and for your mate *will* make a difference. If possible, take time each week (or each day) to pray together with your spouse. If your spouse is not yet a believer, or is not open to praying together (don't push, Popular Sanguines and Powerful Cholerics!), commit to pray for your spouse and your relationship on your own. In the same way that both the husband and the wife will benefit when only one partner acts on his or her understanding of the Personalities, both parties will be blessed when even one member takes the initiative to pray for the relationship (whether the other partner knows *why* or not!).

Take a minute to pray the following prayer for your marriage and your spouse.

Lord, thank You for my husband/wife. Thank You for our marriage and our friendship. You have all wisdom and knowledge as to how to make ours the best possible relationship—one that brings glory to You, blessings to others and joy to each other. That's the kind of marriage I want.

Please help me, Father, to better meet the needs of my spouse. Help me to truly understand his/her Personality and to appreciate the way You've made him/ her. What can I do today to bless him/her? Or maybe I just need to be. Whatever the need, make me sensitive to it, I pray. Make me sensitive to You, Holy Spirit, that I might follow Your perfect leading.

I commit to learning, to listening and to loving. I commit to putting my partner's needs before my own. I also commit to communicating my own needs in a way that is honest and humble. I ask You to heal our marriage where it has suffered brokenness. Show me if I have unknowingly hurt my spouse and help me to make things right. I offer forgiveness, too, for the hurts that I have sustained.

I ask You to bless our marriage. Be the foundation of it. Be the light that shines through it. In Jesus' name, amen.

CHAPTER 7

PARENTING

Physically speaking, parents rarely produce little clones of themselves. The same is true—and often more so—with the little Personalities that parents bring into the world.

Was He/She Born That Way?

If you're a parent, you can probably identify with the bewilderment of the Perfect Melancholy mother whom Marita writes about on page 157 in *Wired That Way*. Perhaps you and your spouse are both strong-willed go-getters and, despite all your efforts, you have an emotional little girl whose sprightly and sensitive nature is beyond your understanding. Or maybe you've always been one to surround yourself with people and activities, only to find yourself baffled by your son who would much rather stay at home playing computer games all day by himself. Or perhaps you're the child and you've always felt like the black sheep of the family—that you never quite measured up to your parents' standards.

Great differences, however, don't have to prohibit great relationships. As with marital relationships, parent-child relationships take work to make them work. And they can work!

• Write out Proverbs 22:6. How does this verse apply to a child's Personality?

• What does Psalm 139:13-16 tell you about God's hand in designing your child's "inmost being"?

Think about your own children or grandchildren, or even about other children whom you know. When you observe them interacting with friends and siblings in their classrooms, on the playground, and in their interactions with you, are they more reclusive or social? More studious or playful? Quiet or chatty? Bossy or easygoing? Can you identify their primary Personalities? Their secondary Personalities?

What Kind of Parent Are You?

Marita says, "Our Personality sets the tone for how we approach parenting" (page 159). Consider your Personality type, and then consider your parenting style (or your teaching style or way of relating to children in general).

• Identify two or three specific ways in which your Personality manifests itself in your parenting style and in the way you relate to your children:

• In which areas do you see your Personality's strengths at work?

• In which do you see your weaknesses?

• In which areas are you frustrated, not knowing why you might be butting heads with your child?

If you often find yourself at odds with your children, there's a good chance that the source of this conflict has more to do with Personality than you may have suspected. It's not just because the child is going through the "terrible twos" (or later, puberty) that you seem to be at odds. And think how much more you'll need an understanding of your child's and your own Personality and emotional needs when he or she does goes through transitional times!

Popular Sanguine Parent

If you're a Popular Sanguine parent, make sure that you are not "stealing the show" from your child. If you are—or if you find that you like to have your kids invite their friends over so that *you* can entertain them—examine your motives. Go through your Emotional Needs Checklist. Do you see any red flags? Are you emotionally malnourished? Have your needs been satisfied in healthy ways? Remember, *you are the parent.* Your child—no matter what his or her personality is—needs *your* attention, not vice versa.

- What does Proverbs 21:23 say about guarding your mouth? How might this apply to an overly expressive Popular Sanguine parent?

- What might some of your Sanguine weaknesses be?

- How can you transform those into strengths in your parenting and use them to bless your family?

Powerful Choleric Parent

Ruth, a Certified Personality Trainer, remembers life with her Powerful Choleric mother:

As a Powerful Choleric, my mother was always busy. I recall one semester of her college career when she worked three jobs in three different towns, went to college full-time, kept house, and helped on the farm while providing for her three children. She started attending college when I was in elementary school (even though she had not finished the eighth grade many years earlier) and finished her college studies in record time, receiving special honors due to her excellent grades. Since I am Popular Sanguine, I always wanted to talk and tell her every detail of what was going on in my life. I remember craving her attention so much and wanting her to just look at me and listen to me. My mother not only did everything well, but she could also do several things at once. But I just wanted her to put whatever she was doing down and look at me so that I would know that she was listening.

In *Wired That Way,* Marita writes, "If Powerful Choleric parents are living in their weaknesses, they might squash their children in the process of getting the job done. If they choose to use their strengths, however, these Powerful Cholerics can give a deep sense of security to their children because they know how to take care of business and can be trusted" (page 162).

- If you are a Powerful Choleric parent, do you see any ways in which you might be "squashing" your child?

- Write out the following Scriptures:

  Psalm 133:1

  Ephesians 6:4

  Colossians 3:21

- What can a Powerful Choleric parent learn from these verses?

- Now reflect on the sidebar "Home Sweet Home" by Karen Kilby on pages 163-164 of *Wired That Way*. How did Karen and her husband, son and daughter-in-law manage to live successfully in the same house for a period of time? How did their understanding of the Personalities lend to their being able to "dwell together in unity"?

Perfect Melancholy Parent

Regarding Perfect Melancholy parents, Marita states, "the Perfect Melancholy parent is what all the others wish they could be: clean, neat, organized, on time, detail-conscious, talented, dedicated, musical, artistic, sensitive, sincere and steadfast. This is great, unless the Perfect Melancholy's child is *not* clean, neat, organized, on time, detail-conscious, talented, dedicated, sensitive, sincere or steadfast. Coming under the critical eye of the Perfect Melancholy parent can be painful" (page 166). Christine tells of a time when she realized this about herself:

> I have read many books on people skills, and I felt that I was making good progress from being a bossy Powerful Choleric/Perfect Melancholy to being someone who at least lifted people up. However, when I was out shopping with my Peaceful Phlegmatic son (who was 19 years old at the time), I realized that I had a ways to go.
>
> I am rather fussy with my coffee, and when it didn't arrive as I had requested, I asked the person behind the counter if she would kindly go back and remake it. Well, my son was so embarrassed. "Now you know why I don't like going out anywhere with you and Dad," he said. "Nothing is ever right or good enough!"
>
> "But didn't I speak kindly to her?" I asked. He agreed, but he still felt that I should have explained to her that I have experience in the hospitality industry and know how to make coffee properly. Don't you just love that peaceful desire in him?
>
> Hence I continue to learn. I didn't realize what an important requirement *respect* was for a Peaceful Phlegmatic.

- Reflecting on the above story and the story of Lynn in *Wired That Way* (see pages 167-169), what could each of these Perfect Melancholy moms have done differently to protect the emotional needs of each child?

- How can Perfect Melancholy parents maintain a personal standard of perfection for themselves and yet extend grace and understanding to their children—especially those children who have less organized or detail-oriented Personalities?

- Look up Ephesians 6:4 and Colossians 3:21. What can Perfect Melancholy parents learn from these verses about not exasperating their children by placing unrealistic expectations upon them?

If you are a Perfect Melancholy parent, you also need to make sure to carve out personal time and space for yourself. Children make life busy—and often quite noisy! It's important that you find healthy ways to meet your needs in order to have the emotional strength to meet your family's needs. It's like putting on the oxygen mask on an airplane—you must get your flow of oxygen going first so that you don't keel over while trying to help your child!

- Look at Jesus' examples in Mark 1:35 and 6:31-32. Even Christ took time away from people and from the demands on Him in order to rest and pray. What's something you can do to incorporate solitude and silence into your daily routine?

Peaceful Phlegmatic Parent

Peaceful Phlegmatic parents tend to be agreeable and easygoing with their children. Because of this, however, their children will often push the boundaries to see just how far they can go. As Marita states, "Being too laid back and always accepting a stance of peace can often create a much bigger problem than if these parents had just dealt with the situation to begin with" (pages 169-171).

• What can a laid-back Peaceful Phlegmatic parent learn from the verse, "He who spares the rod hates his son, but he who loves him is careful to discipline him" (Proverbs 13:24)?

• Even Peaceful Phlegmatic parents have to learn when to extend grace and when to extend the rod, so to speak, in disciplining children. Do you feel you have that appropriate balance in your parenting?

• What can Peaceful Phlegmatics do to establish the boundaries necessary to maintain an appropriate level of authority and respect with their children and, thus, peace in their homes?

• What about a Peaceful Phlegmatic home might be a draw to your children and their friends? How can you, as a parent, use this as an opportunity for sharing Christ?

What Kind of Child Do You Have?

You know what kind of Personality you have and how it might affect those around you. But what about your children or the children with whom you work or are close to? Even from infancy Personalities can be seen, so it shouldn't be hard to detect those of your little ones or teenagers (or adult children!).

Popular Sanguine Child

Popular Sanguine children are energetic, lighthearted and talkative. However, they can have a hard time getting things done if they don't consider those tasks to be enjoyable. They also tend to be a little scatter-brained and have trouble with organization.

- What could you, as an authority figure in your children's life, do to make such tasks as cleaning their room, doing household chores, studying, taking music lessons, or going to the doctor more fun? List a few ideas here.

Sometimes simply talking with a Popular Sanguine child and turning on some upbeat music while trying to accomplish a task can be a real motivator. A big smile of approval and a little bit of silliness can also go a long way with these lighthearted little people. And remember, they need praise and affirmation *frequently*. This doesn't mean that you throw out meaningless flattery, but that you deliberately look for things—even little things—to praise them for.

- If you are not a Popular Sanguine, but have a Popular Sanguine child in your life, have you tried to make his or her Personality more like your own? If so, how?

- What can you start doing now to encourage that child to be who God created him or her to be and to live in his or her strengths?

Perhaps you're not an affectionate person, but your son or daughter—especially if he or she is a Popular Sanguine—might be. In the same way that words don't cost us anything, hugs do not either! So reach out and touch your children. It might be the one simple thing they need to feel that you love and approve of them.

- Write out Matthew 19:13-14. What was Jesus' response to the children who came to Him?

- Do you think He loved and accepted them for who they were?

Powerful Choleric Child

Remember, Powerful Cholerics are motivated by a good challenge. They want a goal to strive after, something to accomplish—something that will win them acknowledgment or reward when it's done.

- What positive challenge can you give your Powerful Choleric child?

- How can you teach your children to be godly winners and graceful *team players* regardless of the outcome?

Focus on the principles found in 1 Corinthians 13:4-7: patience, kindness, humility and an attitude that's not given to anger. Find creative ways of emphasizing these principles to your young Powerful Cholerics while also looking for opportunities to build them up and to meet their emotional needs.

- What responsibility can you give your Powerful Choleric child at home or in the classroom to fulfill his or her need for control?

- Do you see a leader-to-be in your Powerful Choleric child?

- Read the stories of young Joseph in Genesis 37 and of Jesus as a boy in Luke 2:41-52. What can you take from these passages to help you bring up a leadership-oriented child?

Perfect Melancholy Child

With a tendency to be introverted, Perfect Melancholy children can often come across as sullen or antisocial. In their need to be perfect, they might appear to be too nitpicky. It's important, however, not to nag them to become people they are not or to fret over their deep-thinking nature. The parents of the Perfect Melancholy must find ways to support their child and develop his or her strengths.

- What are the Perfect Melancholy child's primary emotional needs?

- In Cheri's story about Michael and his mother (see page 174 in *Wired That Way*), how did his mother violate those needs?

- Does your own child have a tendency not to be very social? If so, what can you do to respect your child's boundaries and needs in this area, yet keep him or her from becoming antisocial or reclusive?

- How can you draw out the deep, passionate nature of the Perfect Melancholy children in your life? Jot down any ideas you come up with for nurturing their creativity and talent.

Peaceful Phlegmatic Child

Marita states, "Many parents of Peaceful Phlegmatics think they have failed because these children have no burning desire to *do* anything. Sitting around is just fine for them. And if their parents in frustration get up and do their work for them, these children will let them" (page 175). Does this sound familiar to you? If so, don't feel discouraged. You most likely have a Peaceful Phlegmatic child on your hands. Now, you have the tools to understand and motivate that child.

- How can the parent of a Peaceful Phlegmatic child teach responsibility and the need to be productive to that child while fostering a sense of self-worth in him or her?

- Have you ever found that you, like Cheri, have catered to a child who is quite capable of doing things for himself or herself?

• What could be the danger of treating your child this way?

• What are some reasonable expectations and rewards you can establish for your Peaceful Phlegmatic child?

• What might be some ways that you, if you're not a Peaceful Phlegmatic, can back off and just allow your children to be themselves?

Putting It into Practice

God has created each of us with our own individual Personalities—including our children. When parents try to change their children instead of encourage them to live in the strength of their Personality, they basically communicate to their children that God doesn't approve of them the way that they are. So, as parents, we need to quit trying to shape our children into our own Personality types and actively seek to understand the unique talents and gifts that God has given to them.

Have you been trying to shape your children into something other than the Personality that God intended them to be? If so, pray this simple prayer.

Father, I need Your help to be a better parent (teacher, aunt, mentor). Thank You for revealing my children's Personalities to me and for giving me insight into how they are wired. I want to grow in my understanding of who they are and what makes them tick. I want Your heart for them: a heart of love and patience that knows when and how to discipline and when and how to encourage. Father God, please give me the grace to meet their emotional needs and to help them grow and mature out of their weaknesses and into their strengths. In Jesus' name, amen.

CHAPTER 8

COMMUNICATION

Language creates barriers between people of different cultures. In the same way, each Personality is somewhat of a culture unto itself. When we learn how to accurately interpret and speak the "language" of another person, we can bridge the Personality barriers that divide us from each other, learn how to communicate more effectively, and build better relationships.

Of course, just understanding how our Personalities influence our communication will not immediately eliminate every problem that we will have with others. However, by understanding our Personality and the Personalities of others, we can use that knowledge to find the root of misunderstandings between ourselves and others and then determine how to fix those problems.

- In *Wired That Way*, Marita tells the story of a time that she cooked an elaborate breakfast for her husband, Chuck (see pages 188-189). When she asked him how his breakfast was, her husband responded with the word "fine." Have you ever had a similar experience?

- Even if you're not a Popular Sanguine, have you ever felt stunned or disappointed by the reaction of another to something special you did for that person? Briefly describe the situation.

- How did the other person's response make you feel?

- Can you attribute this experience to your Personality differences?

- Did Marita and Chuck allow their situation to become tense? How did they diffuse any potential offense?

Marita writes, "Because [Chuck and I] understand each other's Personality and care enough about our relationship to make the extra effort to communicate, we can laugh about things that would otherwise be problematic" (page 189). The key ideas here are *making the extra effort* and *being understanding.* To really create good communication with your partner, coworker, roommate or children, you have to *want* to understand them and be willing to make the extra effort to communicate in their "language."

- Think about your Personality and your inherent communication style. How does your approach to communication impact the people around you?

- Think about the people with whom you come in contact every day. What are their Personalities?

- How can you adjust your approach so that they really hear you when you speak?

The following story sums up how people can learn to communicate in another person's Personality language:

> Written communication is my passion. I teach letter-writing workshops and I always include a segment on the Personalities. After explaining the general concepts, I show examples of what I call inter-Personality communications. The first example is a simple white envelope with the word "Son" written in bold lettering. Inside is a note written with a Sharpie pen that reads:

> *Son,*
>
> *What you did today was difficult. You have a talent for helping your younger brother and sister make peace.*
>
> *Respectfully yours,*
> *Dad*

> I ask my students, "If you were a Peaceful Phlegmatic son and received this note on your pillow from your Powerful Choleric father, what would you think? Do you think the son would keep this letter among his most prized possessions in the years to come?"
>
> The next letter I hold up is in a shiny gold envelope tied with a red satin ribbon to which two large gold jingle bells have been attached. Inside is the following note:

> *Darling,*
>
> *You looked gorgeous last night. You're still the girl I met 32 years ago at the Christmas mixer. Your sparkle and sense of fun attracted me to you. It was either that or your red silk dress and jingle-bell earrings. When we danced the last dance cheek-to-cheek, I knew that I wanted to get to know you better! I never told you before, but when I hear the song "Lady in Red," I think of you.*
>
> *Would you like to dance?*
>
> *Your loving husband*

I then ask my students, "If you were a Popular Sanguine wife who received this note from your Perfect Melancholy husband, what would you think? How would you feel?" Next, I hold up a note on a pad of paper that reads:

Jim,

Mom called. She and Dad will be in town Sunday and will come by about 6:00 P.M. Her cell phone number is 555-1212. We can call to see if they have a change of plans—or if we do.

Love,
Linda

I ask my students, "If you were a Perfect Melancholy husband and received this note from your Popular Sanguine wife, would you feel like she'd made the extra effort to help you plan your day?" I then hold up my last example—a copy of an actual letter on stationery with a cabbage rose border. It is from a Peaceful Phlegmatic/Perfect Melancholy woman to her Popular Sanguine/Powerful Choleric aunt.

The letter is from my friend Mary, who taught me a lot about the heart of letter writing. While Mary was visiting her Aunt Jo, they sat in the kitchen and sipped a cup of tea. Mary asked, "How are you doing since Uncle Hugh died?"

"Mary, this is one thing I miss the most," Aunt Jo replied. "Hugh and I used to share conversation and a cup of tea every afternoon."

Several months after their conversation, Aunt Jo was in poor health and would not be able to attend the wedding of Mary's daughter, Holly. Mary had listened with her Perfect Melancholy heart and remembered her aunt's loneliness. She knew that Aunt Jo was impatient with her illness and heartsick at being the only family member who would miss the marriage celebration.

So a few days after the wedding, Mary sat at her kitchen table. While she drank a cup of tea, her husband crafted a miniature teapot from gift-wrap—pink flowers on a cream-colored background. When he was done, Mary tucked a spiced tea bag inside. Then, on flower-strewn stationery, Mary began a letter to Aunt Jo with these words:

I'm sending this so we can pretend that we are having tea together. Get your china cup and saucer, make a pot of tea and sit down at the kitchen table, while I tell you all about Holly's wedding.

Mary went on to describe the beadwork on the bodice of Holly's wedding gown and the pink dresses Holly had sewn for her two cousin-bridesmaids and her roommate-turned-maid-of-honor. She relayed the family reunion atmosphere created by Aunt Jo's two sisters and numerous nieces and nephews. Mary included snippets of people's reactions, including one aunt's expression of delight in the wedding's simple elegance and the big white dahlias and gladiolus interspersed with babies' breath and other dainty white flowers.

After filling four sheets of stationery with rich detail of the wedding, Mary slipped the paper teapot, a newspaper clipping and a few wedding photos inside the letter with a promise to send more.

In my letter-writing workshops, I then ask, "Which of the four notes above made a positive difference in the lives of the sender and the receiver?" In fact, each of these letters affected the addressee's life, simply because the sender took the time to write the letter in that person's language. In the same way, whether you're speaking—or writing a simple note—you *can* learn to communicate in different Personality languages.

—Linda Jewell

Communication Styles

Let's examine each Personality's style in-depth and learn how those differences affect our communication—and how we can improve it.

Popular Sanguine

What can Popular Sanguines do to improve communication with others? Because Popular Sanguines can talk incessantly (regardless of whether or not anyone is actually listening to them), the first step they can take is to limit their conversation and allow others the opportunity to talk. They can then work to tone down the volume of their voice and actually *listen* to others. And because a hallmark of the Popular Sanguine's communication style is to jump from one topic to another, they can work on focusing on one item of conversation at a time.

- In many situations, why is the Popular Sanguine's talkative nature a positive thing for those around him or her?

- When is the Popular Sanguine's talkative nature a negative thing?

- What are a few things Popular Sanguines can focus on to improve the way they communicate with others?

- Write out each of the following Proverbs. What can the Popular Sanguine learn from each of these?

Proverbs 11:13

Proverbs 12:23

Proverbs 13:3

In Romans 12:3, Paul writes, "For by the grace given me I say to every one of you: Do not think of yourself more highly than you ought, but rather think of yourself with sober judgment, in accordance with the measure of faith God has given you."

- How could this verse apply to a Popular Sanguine who thinks that his or her story is more interesting or entertaining than anyone else's?

- How do you feel when you're telling someone something important or sharing about an exciting experience and that person changes the subject or frequently interjects with his or her own story or experience?

- If you're a Popular Sanguine, here's a project for you:

  — Ask the first question at the beginning of a conversation.

  — Listen without thinking about what you will say next. Keep eye contact with the other person, focusing on what he or she is saying.

  — Verbally reflect on what the other person has said, asking meaningful questions when appropriate.

  — Don't change the subject and don't start talking about yourself or your funny story until the other person invites you to.

Powerful Choleric

The communication style of Powerful Cholerics tends to be brief and to the point. They will often issue commands with little thought for how their words may be perceived by others. Because of this, to improve communication, Powerful Cholerics must take a real interest in others, time the time to make small talk, and ask for what they need from others rather than demand it.

- If you're a Powerful Choleric, have you noticed this about yourself?

- If you're not a Powerful Choleric, have you ever felt offended by a Powerful Choleric who communicated in this way?

- What are a few specific things that you can do to improve your overall communication with others?

We see in the Gospels that Jesus was very approachable. Children, women, Gentiles, outcasts—all came to Him and were received by Him. Though He had a clear-cut mission that He was very focused on fulfilling, and though He spoke His mind boldly at times, He did not brush others aside or leave them feeling insignificant. As natural-born leaders, Powerful Cholerics need to follow the Ultimate Leader's example in communicating with others. They can learn to be both *lions*—bold and powerful and strong—and *lambs*—gentle and able to follow the lead of others when necessary.

- As a Powerful Choleric, do you recognize any relationships in your life in which communication has ceased or the other person has shut down?

- Does the way you communicate with that person have anything to do with the problem? If so, how will you try to repair communication (and any hurt feelings)?

- What does Philippians 4:4-5 tell us to do?

- Are you making your gentleness known to all with whom you communicate?

- If you're a Powerful Choleric, write down the following quote from page 196 of *Wired That Way* on a sheet of paper:

Powerful Cholerics often believe that the time, effort and energy it takes to relate with people don't help the bottom line. However, if they truly want to be more productive, they recognize that the "non-productive" time it takes to ask questions, listen and say a heartfelt thank-you will make you more productive in the long run.

Place the paper where you'll see it often!

Perfect Melancholy

Perfect Melancholies are better at listening than talking, sharing only on a "need to know" basis. Yet they need to realize that they have something to say! As deep thinkers who are intellectually and/or artistically gifted, Perfect Melancholies have much to offer. Their wisdom and sensitivity is a gift to others that cannot be received until given in conversation.

While listening to others is a great attribute of Perfect Melancholies, it can also become a source of self-righteousness and a snare to them if they never give of themselves by *talking*. And Perfect Melancholies need to not be afraid of what others will think when they speak up—as Proverbs 10:11 says, "The mouth of the righteous is a fountain of life."

- If you are a Perfect Melancholy, which of Marita's suggestions struck a chord with you? Do you need to lighten up? Enter into the conversation? Think more positively?

- What do the following verses indicate about having a light touch in your communication with others and in your general attitude toward life?

Psalm 28:7

Psalm 30:11

Proverbs 12:25

Philippians 4:4-6

- Write out—and take a moment to reflect on—1 Thessalonians 5:11 and Hebrews 3:13.

- How can you as a Perfect Melancholy apply these verses in order to become more positive in your communication with others?

Remember, praise is important to several of the other Personalities, so don't be stingy with positive feedback. The more generous you are with verbal encouragement toward others, the more likely they'll be willing to generously meet your emotional needs.

Peaceful Phlegmatic

The Peaceful Phlegmatic is a listener, almost preferring to stay uninvolved—seemingly fearful of entering into conversation. Yet in times of stress, the Peaceful Phlegmatic is the one to talk to, as just the sound of his or her voice is calming.

Unlike Powerful Cholerics, Peaceful Phlegmatics are usually very approachable. They are laid-back and easygoing. Like their Personality opposite, however, they don't communicate or express much, leaving other Personalities guessing at how they really feel and what they really think. Because of this, Peaceful Phlegmatics need to work on opening up to others, expressing their opinions, and not being so low key in their conversations.

- If you're a Peaceful Phlegmatic, resolve to put one of these suggestions for improving communication into action as you interact with others this week. Which suggestion did you choose to incorporate into your life?

Marita writes, "If you are a Peaceful Phlegmatic, learn to be effusive. Muster up all the superlatives you can think of . . . if other people feel discouraged by your lack of interest, they will eventually discontinue their interaction with you" (page 199).

- How is Romans 12:15, "Rejoice with those who rejoice; mourn with those who mourn," a challenge to nonresponsive communication?

- How is it a *loving* act for a Peaceful Phlegmatic to express his or her opinion or desires when asked by a family member, close friend or colleague?

If you're a Peaceful Phlegmatic, here's a challenge for you: share your faith. While some people distinctly possess the gift of evangelism, all Christians are called to give voice to the good news. However, because you are a Peaceful Phlegmatic and tend to be more on the mellow side, you may find it difficult to actively and confidently lead others to the truth. So take steps today to consciously open up to become a better communicator of your faith in Christ. See your quiet, mellow Personality as an invitation to those who might ordinarily feel threatened by Christians whom they perceive to be loud, "in your face" types. Welcome them. Make the most of every opportunity.

- While it's easy to notice and be critical of those who have Personalities that are the opposite of your own, make a point of observing others who share your Personality type. What weaknesses do they display? What strengths? How can you learn from their communication style to improve your own?

Making Communication More Effective

As Marita says, "Whether your communication is professional or personal, you will find it enhanced by following the basic communication tips for your Personality and then changing your approach to meet the needs of others. You cannot change other people, but you can change the way you approach them" (page 202). Let's examine some of the different ways that individuals with one Personality can better communicate with those who have different Personalities.

Popular Sanguine

When speaking with Powerful Cholerics, keep your conversation to the point—*especially* if you work for one.

- Look up Proverbs 14:23. How does this verse capture the motto that Powerful Cholerics live by?

When talking to a Perfect Melancholy, you need to be sensitive to his or her schedule and level of interest.

- Why is this important to a Perfect Melancholy?

- For those of you who are Popular Sanguines, if you really want to share something, but the timing isn't right for the Perfect Melancholy you want to share with, what can you do?

When conversing with Peaceful Phlegmatics, remember that they need encouragement and acceptance for who they are, not just for what others think they should be.

- What ways, other than speaking to them, can you communicate how much you value and appreciate the Peaceful Phlegmatics in your life?

Powerful Choleric

When speaking with Popular Sanguines (or, rather, when they're talking *to* you), make it a point to show *interest* in the conversation.

- Look up Philippians 2:3-7. What does this verse say about how you should treat people with Personalities different from your own? What does this passage say about being a "servant," like Christ?

When conversing with a Perfect Melancholy, you will need to resist your natural tendency to listen just long enough to get the gist of the topic and then move on, for doing so will shut down communication with that individual.

- How does the Powerful Choleric's "moving on" mentality affect the Perfect Melancholy?

- How might such an approach be hurtful to someone trying to express an important idea or personal feeling?

When talking to Peaceful Phlegmatics, you will probably again be inclined to rush them to get to the point. In this case, you need to work on developing patience and good listening skills.

- Read Ephesians 4:2 again. Why is this verse so important to remember when communicating with a Peaceful Phlegmatic?

Perfect Melancholy

Marita writes, "When a Perfect Melancholy is talking to a Popular Sanguine, this combination is especially problematic, since the former specializes in criticism and the latter craves praise" (page 208).

- Keeping the Popular Sanguine's needs in mind, what are a few specific things that you can do to foster positive communication?

- How can you graciously set boundaries so that your listening ear doesn't get abused, leaving you feeling resentful?

When communicating with Powerful Cholerics, remember that their time is valuable to them and that they will want to hear just the essentials. You may have to choose to not be offended when the Powerful Cholerics in your life seem to want to keep the conversation brief.

- What will help Powerful Cholerics to hear you best?

- How should you express what you want to communicate?

Keep it positive when speaking with Peaceful Phlegmatics. You will have to suppress your ability to spot the negatives in your Peaceful Phlegmatic friends and neighbors, and look for ways to offer them praise.

- Look up Colossians 4:6. Why is this verse a good rule of thumb to follow when conversing with a Peaceful Phlegmatic?

- Think of someone you know who is a Peaceful Phlegmatic. What encouraging words can you say to that person this week?

Peaceful Phlegmatic

Peaceful Phlegmatics are the ones who will have to stretch themselves the most to make conversation, which is especially problematic when dealing with Popular Sanguines (who live for a good talk). Even if you genuinely like someone and enjoy his or her company, that person will never know it if you don't express interest.

- What are some specific things you can do to foster healthy communication with Popular Sanguines?

- What are some nonverbal expressions you can give to show them that you care?

- How can you show excitement when they come to you with creative ideas—no matter how phony it might feel for you?

Don't shrink back when in conversation with a Powerful Choleric. Let your words be quick and to the point, but don't feel that you have to communicate exactly like the Powerful Choleric in order to get your ideas across.

- Write out Proverbs 12:18. How does this represent the contrast between the ways the Powerful Choleric and the Peaceful Phlegmatic communicate?

- On pages 210-211 of *Wired That Way*, Marita suggests the following for learning how to best communicate to a Powerful Choleric: "Practice reading a paragraph and time yourself. Then read it again and try to cut 25 percent off of your reading time. Then read it again, aiming for a 50 percent decrease." Try this with a Powerful Choleric you know this week.

Perfect Melancholies appreciate facts and documentation. Because of this, you may need to carefully think through the information that you are presenting to people of this Personality type.

- Why should you prepare well before discussing an important matter with a Perfect Melancholy at work?

- Perfect Melancholies and Peaceful Phlegmatics both have a naturally quiet nature. What can you do to be the first one to initiate conversation with your Perfect Melancholy colleagues, family and friends?

Putting It into Practice

Evaluate your specific communication strengths and weaknesses. Consider the Personalities you communicate best with and those whom you'd rather ignore. Ask the Lord to help you be more like Him in all of your interactions with all types of people, and especially with those you're close to. Write a simple prayer here and use it as a reference point for checking your progress from time to time.

CHAPTER 9

THE WORKPLACE

"It has been shown that when people enjoy their jobs, they tend to be more productive, are absent less, and are less likely to move to another job," Marita writes (page 213 of *Wired That Way*). The better suited our jobs are to our Personalities, the more we will enjoy those jobs and want to give our all. In addition, the more we like our employers and coworkers (and the more they like us), the easier and more enjoyable our jobs will be.

Sometimes, liking others and being liked are difficult when working with those who communicate differently from the way that we do. However, by understanding and responding appropriately to individual Personality types and communication styles, and by grasping which work environments cause our own soul to thrive, we are more likely to be happy and successful in our work and with our coworkers.

- Do you enjoy your current job?

- What are your relationships like with your boss (or employees, if you're the boss) and your colleagues?

- Do you think your Personality is a good match for your particular position?

- Describe a work situation in which you felt (or perhaps *feel*, if you're still in it) inadequate and/or unappreciated by your boss or colleagues.

- Or, if you're the boss, do you have or have you ever had an employee who annoys you, who can't seem to "get it" or do the job the way you want it done?

- Given what you now know about the Personalities, what could you have done, or what can you do, to change things?

In *Wired That Way*, Marita tells the story of how she tailored her Popular Sanguine administrative assistant's job description (along with the job descriptions of the rest of her staff) to better fit her Personality style.

- What might be the benefits of making the job to fit the person, rather than vice versa?

- If you are a business owner, manager, recruiter or leader of a ministry or volunteer organization, have you ever considered "behavior-based hiring"?

• What impact would this have on your organization or business? What advantages might there be?

Consider Marita's thoughts: "While the best option is to hire the right Personality for the job, why not make adjustments after the fact? With the cost of training, isn't it worth making employees happy by allowing them to work in their strengths rather than forcing them to do something that goes against their giftings?" (page 215).

• In Steve Robbins's story, "Teambuilding 'The Personalities' Way," what challenges did his new team of three face?

• What did he do to remedy the situation?

• What have been the results of his strategic advising and team building?

• Do you see a situation similar to this in your work environment? If so, what are the Personalities of the key players involved?

Write out an action plan for how you can put your knowledge of the Personalities into action. You might have to be discreet about it, knowing that you can't be too pushy with certain individuals involved, or you might be able to openly share what you know about each Personality's strengths and weaknesses. You might even be able to get everyone to read *Wired That Way!*

How Does Each Personality Function at Work?

Popular Sanguine

Popular Sanguines are naturally creative people and are happiest in jobs that allow for a diversity of tasks, interaction with people, and room for creativity.

- What do Popular Sanguines need *lots* of (on the job and everywhere)?

- If you work with a Popular Sanguine, what are some specific ways that can you offer praise and approval for his or her performance?

- Popular Sanguines are prone to chat and get distracted with personal issues at work. How do the following verses speak to the issue of doing work with excellence and integrity at all times—not merely when the boss is looking?

Proverbs 14:2

Colossians 3:22

• Do you recognize any personal work habits that need shaping up?

• What warning does Marita give the Popular Sanguine in regard to being "too cute" in the workplace?

Take these admonitions to heart, Popular Sanguines, but also be *free to be fun*! Two Popular Sanguine strengths are the ability to make work feel like play and the desire to encourage others on the job. If this is you, don't hide your light behind your desk—let it shine! Use your naturally warm Personality to brighten the office and bring a smile to colleagues and clients alike. But remember to do it all in a spirit of maturity, keeping the best interests of others in mind. *Bless*—not *overwhelm*—them. And if you're not a Popular Sanguine, don't be a Scrooge! Allow the lighthearted flare and creative style of a Popular Sanguine inspire and uplift you.

Powerful Choleric

If you are a Powerful Choleric, learn to be a team player. Be careful of the "if I can't win, then I won't play" or the "if I can't lead, then I won't do it" attitude. Use your leadership gifts to bless others and to get the job done. And remember, God wants you to get it done *together* with the rest of the team. As Paul prayed, "May the God who gives [*you, the Powerful Choleric*] endurance and encouragement give you a *spirit of unity* among yourselves as you follow Christ Jesus" (Romans 15:5, emphasis added).

• Read Acts 27. How was Paul's Powerful Choleric side demonstrated in this situation?

• What ideas can you take from Paul in regard to motivating others and solving problems that involve a group or an entire organization?

Another man, who briefly yet poignantly graces the pages of the Bible, also has something to teach us about leadership—about being a leader *under authority*. Read his story in Luke 7:1-10.

• What can we learn about authority from the Centurion's attitude?

Just as powerful horses need to be bridled and controlled by a skillful rider, so Powerful Cholerics need to keep a rein on their fast-paced activity. They need to let God harness their strengths, lest they become weaknesses that cause strain—and even destruction—in work relationships.

• Write out Ephesians 4:2. If you're a Powerful Choleric, how can you translate this into your work style?

• Write out Proverbs 16:24 and 22:11. What do these verses speak to you about how you should relate to others at work?

Remember, Powerful Cholerics, that your confident, authoritative nature often intimidates others, causing them to shrink back or shut down. Taking the time to receive input from those with whom you work and to speak to them with grace and patience and in a pleasant tone will help win them over. Just that minor investment could gain you the sense of loyalty that you need and the productivity that you desire from a team.

Perfect Melancholy
At various times throughout the Old Testament, God reveals Himself as a Perfect Melancholy. He gives detailed directions to Noah for the engineering of the Ark, meticulous measurements to Moses for the construction of the tabernacle, and intricate instructions to Solomon for the building of the Temple.

- Being detail-oriented is a gift from God. If you're a Perfect Melancholy, how can you use this gift to benefit your company or organization?

- If you are an employer or a colleague of a Perfect Melancholy, what can you do to encourage, utilize and appreciate his or her detail-oriented nature and organizational strengths?

- Establishing a "history of excellence and accuracy" will win you trust and respect in the work world. What does Proverbs 22:29 say about this?

We can also learn from the Perfect Melancholy how to be sensitive to the needs of others. We see this reflected in Curt's story on page 228 of *Wired That Way*.

- What did Curt do in the case of the chronically late X-ray technician?

- How did his solution to the problem demonstrate sensitivity to the needs of her personal life as well as to the needs of the department?

- How might a Powerful Choleric have responded in this same situation? A Peaceful Melancholy?

On the other hand, in their weakness, Perfect Melancholies tend to be too critical, placing the same expectation for perfection on others as they do on themselves.

- How can an overly critical attitude damage relationships and decrease productivity?

- Write out the following verses. What warning do they give about being overly critical of others?

  Matthew 7:1-2

  Romans 14:10

  James 2:12-13

If you're a Perfect Melancholy manager or leader of some sort, think of ways that you can "staff your weaknesses" by hiring other Personalities (especially Popular Sanguines) to bring balance to your business, organization or department.

Peaceful Phlegmatic

Although Jesus was often in the spotlight and spoke confidently to the masses, He also served unselfishly and without need for applause. The same supportive, glad-to-serve spirit can be seen in the Peaceful Phlegmatic. In *Wired That Way*, Marita highlights this in her story about Linda, her executive director (see page 231).

- What makes Linda the ideal support person for Marita?

- In what ways might a successful business owner or pastor benefit from having a Peaceful Phlegmatic on his or her team?

- Do you have any support people who quietly serve and keep the peace at your workplace? What do you appreciate most about them?

- Ephesians 4:3 says, "Make every effort to keep the unity of the Spirit through the bond of peace." (Who better to help us do that than the Peaceful Phlegmatic?!) How did Brooke, Sylvia's personal assistant, exemplify this verse in the midst of a stressful million-dollar transaction (see page 232 in *Wired That Way*)?

Peaceful Phlegmatics, however, might be lacking in the areas of discipline, decision-making and productivity.

- What do the following Proverbs have to say about cultivating an attitude of diligence and discipline at work?

Proverbs 10:4

Proverbs 12:24

Proverbs 13:4

- If you are a Peaceful Phlegmatic, what key things can you do to improve your overall performance in your job or volunteer position? (Increase motivation? Build enthusiasm? Develop management skills? Speak up?) Write down one or two, and include a brief statement about how you will practically work them out.

As Peaceful Phlegmatics grow in emotional and spiritual maturity, they can grow in these attributes as well. Combining these skills with their laidback, friendly nature will continue to make them everyone's favorite people to work with!

Putting It into Practice

Marita states, "As you look around your place of work, the groups in which you are a member, or the committees on which you serve, take note of how the Personalities play into happiness on the job, successful team building, and good relationships with clients and customers" (pages 234-235).

- Imagine a Perfect Melancholy, Popular Sanguine, Peaceful Phlegmatic and Powerful Choleric all working together in unison on a given project. What roles might each have and what would be the strengths of this quartet? What would be the potential challenges?

- What are the Personalities that you work with?

- Now that you understand your coworkers, how will you apply this information to improve your relationship with them and make the workplace more functional?

- If you are the boss, can you make some changes to allow your staff to function in the areas in which they are more naturally gifted?

- What do you need from a job in order for your work to be satisfying?

As Marita concludes, "Think about what you need to do to find a job that fits who you are. Now, do it. After all, you spend more waking hours at work that any other single place. Wouldn't it be nice to be happy there?" (page 235).

CHAPTER 10

SPIRITUAL LIFE

Our Personalities play out even in our spiritual lives. Some of us are more given to study, some to one-on-one accountability, and others to abandoned worship. We all have our unique ways in which we seek God, but the key is that *we seek Him*! Maybe you're not into reading the Bible cover to cover or have never quite got into having a quiet time in the morning, preferring instead to spend time with God late at night. That's okay! Very little is *prescribed* in the Bible as to specific methods for cultivating our relationship with God and our spiritual growth. But many examples are given to us throughout the Word. For example:

- The Psalmists write about praising Him with various kinds of instruments, with loud voices and with dancing, and about seeking Him with fasting (see Psalm 150).
- Jesus gives us an example of a simple prayer to "Our Father in Heaven" (see Matthew 6:9-13).
- The Lord gave us an example of extended fasting when He went into the desert, and He retreated regularly to quiet places where He would pray (see Matthew 4:1-4; Mark 6:31,46).
- We're told to worship God in Spirit and in truth (see John 4:24).
- In the book of Acts, we see the disciples meeting together daily for prayer and fellowship. They ate together, laid hands on one another, spoke in tongues and prophesied, and admonished each other.

So, there are many ways in which to worship the Lord and fellowship with one another. There are many Personality combinations that influence the various ways in which each person walks out his or her faith in Christ. Rather than imposing our religious routines and traditions on others, really "only one thing is needed," as Jesus told Martha in Luke 10:42. That "one thing" is the longing to be close to God and to have a heart that desires *Him* above all else.

• Do you have that *one thing?*

• Have you ever felt inadequate as a Christian? Why?

• Do you regularly seek to spend time with the Lord and in His Word?

• If so, do you do so more out of a sense of *duty* or of *desire*?

If not, your Personality is not an excuse. While *how* you spend time with the Lord may look different from the next Christian, it is impossible to really know God and grow into a mature believer without putting your faith into action. If you find prayer and reading the Word to be drudgery, or feel that you just can't get close to God or don't know how to study the Bible, ask your pastor or another trusted Christian to help you.

If you find yourself seeking God out of a sense of duty, ask Him to renew the desire within you to fellowship with Him. Shake up your routine a little—make your approach a bit more spontaneous (or structured, if you're becoming flaky)—to put the joy back into your time with the Lord.

View of God

Our view of God can be shaped or skewed by many things: our upbringing, the church in which we were raised (or having no church background at all), our cultural influences and, of course, our Personalities.

• How do *you* view God? Do you see Him more as friend, Father, someone to be feared, a controller, a comforter?

• How might those who have had bad relationships with (or abuse from) their father figures find it difficult to see God as a loving Father?

While viewing God as a loving Father or a best friend comes naturally for Popular Sanguines, not everyone can easily accept this view. The following story from Cheri illustrates how two different Personalities can respond differently to the same concept.

> Last summer, I heard a zealous Melancholy/Choleric preacher. He was speaking against the idea of "cheap grace" and focusing on the importance of obedience. Perhaps for shock value, he pounded on the pulpit and shouted, "There are too many who will tell you that God accepts you just the way you are. Well, I am here to tell you that is a lie! God does not accept you just the way you are! He *cannot* accept you just the way you are!"
>
> This statement hit me full force, sending my mind and emotions reeling. I tried to stay calm and logically follow where the preacher was going with his concepts. But grief welled up from a very core place in me, and soon I was overwhelmed with tears.
>
> Later, my Perfect Melancholy husband asked me, "What was that all about?" I tried to tell him how shattering it was for me to hear the words, "God does not accept you just the

way you are," as my entire life has been built on the idea that God does love me just the way I am. He shrugged and said, "Actually, I thought the preacher made several very interesting points tonight." Then he added, "You're probably the only person there tonight who interpreted the speaker the way you did."

Perhaps. But I'm pretty sure that if I'd done an exit poll that night, I would have found a bunch of traumatized fellow Popular Sanguines, desperately in need of hugs and a few reassuring rounds of "Jesus Loves Me"!

- Write out the following verses:

  Isaiah 30:18

  John 16:27

  1 John 3:1

- What do these verses reveal about the reality of our Father God's heart toward you?

- Read John 15:15 and 21:12. Would you say Jesus was a friend to His disciples? Do you consider Him your friend?

- Why is it appropriate to fear God? Write down three verses from Scripture that support your answer.

- Would you say that Jesus has absolute authority in your life—that you're living completely under His Lordship?

- Regardless of your Personality type, examine who really has control in your life—you or God. If it's you, what's holding you back from handing over all control to the Lord?

- Why should we want God to be in control of our lives?

- How has God shown Himself to be the Comforter in your life?

- What are some of the names given to Jesus in Isaiah 9:6 that support your Personality's view of God?

Spiritual Strengths

Some of the most prevalent spiritual themes in the Bible are related to grace, knowledge, justification and the sovereignty of God. Each of these themes (or "spiritual strengths") is reflected in the Personalities: to Popular Sanguines, *grace* is a natural extension of God's love; Perfect Melancholies are attracted to the spiritual strength of *knowledge;* Powerful Cholerics embody the spiritual strength of *justification* and works; and Peaceful Phlegmatics have an easy time accepting the *sovereignty of God* in their lives

- What aspect of spiritual strength, of the four that Marita highlights, would you say that you are strongest in?

- Read *The New Unger's Bible Dictionary* definition of "grace" on page 244 of *Wired That Way*. According to this definition, what would you say are the elements of grace that are most attractive to the Popular Sanguine?

- How can a Popular Sanguine use his or her strength in the area of grace?

- Read James 2:14-26. Why is it important, regardless of our Personality, to support our faith with works?

- How can the Powerful Choleric use his or her strength in the area of justification?

- Read Proverbs 2:1-6. What do these verses say about pursuing knowledge?

• How can a Perfect Melancholy use his or strength in the area of the knowledge of God and the Word to bring truth to the world (unbelievers) and to edify the Church (other believers)?

• Why do Peaceful Phlegmatics have an easier time accepting the sovereignty of God in their lives?

• Reread Acts 17:24 -27. Understanding God's sovereignty is foundational to the Christian life. What advantage does one who really grasps and lives his or her life according to this truth have over those who don't?

Growing Closer to God

Marita states, "As Christians, we all desire to grow in our spiritual life and have a closer relationship with God. But what works for one person may not work for another. This is why many of the popular methods for helping people grow in their spirituality—such as reading through the Bible in a year or recording prayers in a journal—produce more spiritual guilt than spiritual growth" (page 248).

• Look up 2 Corinthians 3:17 and Galatians 5:1. How might these verses speak to Popular Sanguines?

• What does Jesus say in Matthew 18:3 about having a childlike heart? How might His words be a draw to non-Christian Popular Sanguines who have been put off by the "stuffiness" of religious behavior?

- What tips does Marita give to the Popular Sanguine for invigorating spiritual growth? How can Popular Sanguines incorporate prayer and Scripture meditation into the activities of their life?

- What tools does Marita suggest that Powerful Cholerics use to aid their spiritual growth?

- What benefits does a one-on-one accountability/prayer partner relationship have? What are the drawbacks?

- Marita writes, "The techniques that work the best [for Powerful Cholerics] in developing their spiritual life are participatory, not passive" (page 251). In what ways can Powerful Cholerics make their spiritual life more active and, thus, more fulfilling? How can you do this for someone whom you are discipling?

- How can Perfect Melancholies make their walk with God more authentic and personal and less rigid and predictable?

- Do you recognize any areas in your spiritual life in which you need to relax perfectionist standards?

- Do you need to repent for placing any such expectations on others?

- Marita writes, "While the Popular Sanguines and Powerful Cholerics are buzzing around in busyness and the Perfect Melancholy is digging deeper, the Peaceful Phlegmatic is basking in God's presence." How is this basking a wonderful thing? (Remember what Jesus said to Martha in Luke 10:38-42.)

- What do the following Scriptures have to say about really pondering the Word?

  Psalm 1:2

  Psalm 119:97,99,148

  Psalm 145:5

- If you're a Peaceful Phlegmatic, how can you keep from feeling paralyzed by routine and ritual and yet remain consistent in fostering your spiritual growth?

Pam sums up well how all of our Personalities fit in the grand scheme of God's plan: "When we are all living Spirit-filled lives and we come together in our strengths, we as a group are like Christ. This is how we, as Christians, are intended to function. No one has every skill or strength. But as we come together, we make a whole, complete in Him" (page 264 of *Wired That Way*).

Spiritual Gifts

In *Wired That Way*, Marita suggests that each Personality has a predisposition toward specific spiritual gifts, and that these gifts are simply extensions of the inherent personality traits in a person. Take a few minutes to read and reflect on the four Bible passages that Marita includes in the section on spiritual gifts:

Romans 12:3-8

1 Corinthians 12:1,4-11,28-30

Ephesians 4:3-6,11-12

1 Peter 4:11

Now, look at the two groups into which Marita divides the gifts (speaking and serving).

• Which of the gifts that Marita lists do you believe that you possess?

• How do these gifts relate to the strengths of your Personality?

• Marita states that "God bestows some gifts that appear in a person regardless of his or her personality type—but this seems to be the exception rather than the rule" (page 256). Has God ever supernaturally equipped you to do something that was completely outside of your comfort zone?

• How are you using the gifts that God has given you to help others?

The Personality of Jesus

Sylvia Jackson, a Certified Personality Trainer, shares the following story about the nature of God:

> I held a weekly connect group meeting in my home. Each week, we would focus on a different element of the Personalities. One week, the topic was how our Personality affects our view of God and consequently our relationship with Him.
>
> Everyone present explained their idea of who God is, how they feel about Him, and how they think He feels about them. I made notes as they spoke, and the results were both surprising and enlightening.
>
> All those who were popular Sanguines talked (a lot) about how they feel God always shows them how much He loves them by all the little things He constantly does. They called Him "Daddy" and talked about how when they prayed, they felt like they were sitting in His lap and telling Him everything—that He was a God of forgiveness. In other words, He gave them His undivided attention, affection and approval.
>
> The Powerful Cholerics said that God has so much for them to do, that He has created them for a destiny and a future, and that they were busy accomplishing it. They talked about how logical God is and how things are orderly in His kingdom. They spoke of God in terms of a counselor and a judge.

Next were the Perfect Melancholies. Their view of God was one of judgment—how disappointed they were with their own spirituality. They knew God wanted them to be better and to do more. Although they were aware of His love and forgiveness, they were also acutely aware that there was a line to be towed and that very few Christians were towing it. Also, more than the other Personalities, they seemed to be aware of the work of the enemy.

The Peaceful Phlegmatics were rather relaxed in their view of God. They felt that He loved them, and they seemed to focus on times of prayer and study, which were very peaceful and restful. They talked about His kindness, mercy and grace.

When everyone was finished sharing, I categorized their responses according to the different Personalities of those attending. We saw for ourselves how God contains all four Personalities, and how we shortchange Him, thinking He is like us. We limit our view of Him according to our own Personality, thereby limiting our faith in who He is and what He will do for us if we will only believe.

The exercise gave us a more complete picture of His Personality and character and opened our hearts to more fully experience Him in ways we had never before considered.

—Sylvia Jackson

As Sylvia mentions, "God contains all four Personalities." In the same way, Jesus was unique in that He embodied the strengths of all four Personalities, but the weaknesses of none.

- How did Jesus reflect each of the Personalities? Cite specific scriptural references to support your answers.

- What is the ultimate goal of every Christian?

- As we grow and mature in Christ, we take on more of the strengths of each Personality and shed more of our Personality's weaknesses. What is one strength that you see in another Personality (and in Jesus!) that you wish to possess?

- Which of your own weaknesses will you commit to working on diminishing?

Putting It into Practice

Reflect on all that you've learned in this study and how you want to use your new knowledge and understanding to better enjoy your relationship with God, love others, and be the amazing individual He has created you to be. Take a moment to pray and ask the Lord to help you with this.

Close by *listening*. God has something to say to each one of us. He is the Author and Perfecter of our faith and the Creator and Lover of our souls—and our Personalities! He wants to use all of our gifts and unique Personality traits to bring glory to Himself and to bring others into relationship with Him. Trust Him to use and refine your Personality and make you a shining light in His kingdom.